thai & chinese
Simple Cookery

STAR
FIRE

This is a Starfire book
First published in 2001

02 04 05 03

3 5 7 9 10 8 6 4

Starfire is part of
The Foundry Creative Media Company Limited
Crabtree Hall, Crabtree Lane, Fulham, London, SW6 6TY

Visit the Foundry website: www.foundry.co.uk/recipes

ISBN: 1-903817-07-2

The CIP record for this book is available from the British Library.

Printed in China

ACKNOWLEDGEMENTS

Authors: Catherine Atkinson, Juliet Barker, Carol Tennant,
Liz Martin, Mari Mererid Williams and Elizabeth Wolf-Cohen
Editorial Consultant: Gina Steer
Project Editor: Karen Fitzpatrick
Photography: Colin Bowling and Paul Forrester
Home Economists and Stylists: Jacqueline Bellefontaine,
Mandy Phipps, Vicki Smallwood and Penny Stephens
Design Team: Helen Courtney, Jennifer Bishop, Lucy Bradbury and Chris Herbert

All props supplied by Barbara Stewart at Surfaces

NOTE
Recipes using uncooked eggs should be avoided by infants,
the elderly, pregnant women and anyone suffering from an illness.

Special thanks to everyone involved in this book, particularly
Karen Fitzpatrick and Gina Steer.

CONTENTS

SOUPS & STARTERS

FISH & SHELLFISH

MEAT

POULTRY

VEGETABLES

ENTERTAINING

HYGIENE IN THE KITCHEN

It is well worth remembering that many foods can carry some form of bacteria. In most cases, the worst it will lead to is a bout of food poisoning or gastroenteritis, although for certain groups this can be more serious – the risk can be reduced or eliminated by good food hygiene and proper cooking.

Do not buy food that is past its sell-by date and do not consume any food that is past its use-by date. When buying food, use the eyes and nose. If the food looks tired, limp or a bad colour or it has a rank, acrid or simply bad smell, do not buy or eat it under any circumstances.

Do take special care when preparing raw meat and fish. A separate chopping board should be used for each; wash the knife, board and the hands thoroughly before handling or preparing any other food.

Regularly clean, defrost and clear out the refrigerator or freezer – it is worth checking the packaging to see exactly how long each product is safe to freeze.

Avoid handling food if suffering from an upset stomach as bacteria can be passed through food preparation.

Dish cloths and tea towels must be washed and changed regularly. Ideally use disposable cloths, which should be replaced on a daily basis. More durable cloths should be left to soak in bleach, then washed in the washing machine on a boil wash.

Keep the hands, cooking utensils and food preparation surfaces clean and do not allow pets to climb on to any work surfaces.

BUYING

Avoid bulk buying where possible, especially fresh produce such as meat, poultry, fish, fruit and vegetables unless buying for the freezer. Fresh foods lose their nutritional value rapidly so buying a little at a time minimises loss of nutrients. It also eliminates a packed refrigerator, which reduces the effectiveness of the refrigeration process.

When buying prepackaged goods such as cans or pots of cream and yogurts, check that the packaging is intact and not damaged or pierced at all. Cans should not be dented, pierced or rusty. Check the sell-by dates even for cans and packets of dry ingredients such as flour and rice. Store fresh foods in the refrigerator as soon as possible – not in the car or the office.

When buying frozen foods, ensure that they are not heavily iced on the outside and the contents feel completely frozen. Ensure that the frozen foods have been stored in the cabinet at the correct storage level and the temperature is below -18°C/-4°F. Pack in cool bags to transport home and place in the freezer as soon as possible after purchase.

PREPARATION

Make sure that all work surfaces and utensils are clean and dry. Hygiene should be given priority at all times.

Separate chopping boards should be used for raw and cooked meats, fish and vegetables. Currently, a variety of good-quality plastic boards come in various designs and colours. This makes differentiating easier and the plastic has the added hygienic advantage of being washable at high temperatures in the dishwasher. (NB: If using the board for fish, first wash in cold water, then in hot to prevent odour!) Also, remember that knives and utensils should always be cleaned thoroughly after use.

When cooking, be particularly careful to keep cooked and raw food separate to avoid any contamination. It is worth washing all fruits and vegetables regardless of whether they are going to be eaten raw or lightly cooked. This rule should apply even to pre-washed herbs and salads.

Do not reheat food more than once. If using a microwave, always check that the food is piping hot all the way through. (In theory, the food should reach 70°C/158°F and needs to be cooked at that temperature for at least three minutes to ensure that all bacteria are killed.)

All poultry must be thawed thoroughly before using, including chicken and poussin. Remove the food to be thawed from the freezer and place in a shallow dish to contain the juices. Leave the food in the refrigerator until it is thawed completely. A 1.4 kg/3 lb whole chicken will take about 26–30 hours to thaw. To speed up the process immerse the chicken in cold water. However, make sure that the water is changed regularly. When the joints can move freely and no ice crystals remain in the cavity, the bird is thawed completely.

Once thawed, remove the wrapper and pat the chicken dry. Place the chicken in a shallow dish, cover lightly and store as close to the base of the refrigerator as possible. The chicken should be cooked as soon as possible.

Some foods can be cooked from frozen including many prepacked foods such as soups, sauces, casseroles and breads. Where applicable follow the manufacturers' instructions.

Vegetables and fruits can also be cooked from frozen, but meats and fish should be thawed first. The only time food can be refrozen is when the food has been thawed thoroughly then cooked. Once the food has cooled, then it can be frozen again. On such occasions the food can only be stored for one month.

All poultry and game (except for duck) must be cooked thoroughly. When cooked, the juices will run clear from the thickest part of the bird – the best area to try is usually the thigh. Other meats, like minced meat and pork should be cooked right the way through. Fish should turn opaque, be firm in texture and break easily into large flakes.

When cooking leftovers, make sure they are reheated until piping hot and that any sauce or soup reaches boiling point first.

STORING
REFRIGERATING AND FREEZING

Meat, poultry, fish, seafood and dairy products should all be refrigerated. The temperature of the refrigerator should be between 1–5°C/34–41°F while the freezer temperature should not rise above -18°C/-4°F.

To ensure the optimum refrigerator and freezer temperature, avoid leaving the door open for a long time. Try not to overstock the refrigerator as this reduces the airflow inside and affects the effectiveness in cooling the food within.

When refrigerating cooked food, leave it to cool down quickly and completely before refrigerating. Hot food will raise the temperature of the refrigerator and possibly affect or spoil other food stored in it.

Food within the refrigerator and freezer should always be covered. Raw and cooked food should be stored in separate parts of the refrigerator. Cooked food should be kept on the top shelves of the refrigerator, while raw meat, poultry and fish should be placed on bottom shelves to avoid drips and cross-contamination. It is recommended that eggs should be refrigerated in order to maintain their freshness and shelf life.

Take care that frozen foods are not stored in the freezer for too long. Blanched vegetables can be stored for one month; beef, lamb, poultry and pork for six months and unblanched vegetables and fruits in syrup for a year. Oily fish and sausages should be stored for three months. Dairy products can last four to six months while cakes and pastries should be kept in the freezer for three to six months.

HIGH-RISK FOODS

Certain foods may carry risks to people who are considered vulnerable such as the elderly, the ill, pregnant women, babies, young infants and those suffering from a recurring illness.

It is advisable to avoid those foods listed below which belong to a higher-risk category.

There is a slight chance that some eggs carry the bacteria salmonella. Cook the eggs until both the yolk and the white are firm to eliminate this risk. Pay particular attention to dishes and products incorporating lightly cooked or raw eggs, which should be eliminated from the diet. Sauces including Hollandaise, mayonnaise, mousses, soufflés and meringues all use raw or lightly cooked eggs, as do custard-based dishes, ice creams and sorbets. These are all considered high-risk foods to the vulnerable groups mentioned above.

Certain meats and poultry also carry the potential risk of salmonella and so should be cooked thoroughly until the juices run clear and there is no pinkness left. Unpasteurised products such as milk, cheese (especially soft cheese), pâté, meat (both raw and cooked) all have the potential risk of listeria and should be avoided.

When buying seafood, buy from a reputable source, which has a high turnover to ensure freshness. Fish should have bright clear eyes, shiny skin and bright pink or red gills. The fish should feel stiff to the touch, with a slight smell of sea air and iodine. The flesh of fish steaks and fillets should be translucent with no signs of discoloration. Molluscs such as scallops, clams and mussels are sold fresh and are still alive. Avoid any that are open or do not close when tapped lightly. In the same way, univalves such as cockles or winkles should withdraw back into their shells when prodded lightly.

When choosing cephalopods such as squid and octopus they should have a firm flesh and pleasant sea smell.

As with all fish, whether it is shellfish or seafish, care is required when freezing it. It is imperative to check whether the fish has been frozen before. If it has been frozen, then it should not be frozen again under any circumstances.

FRESH INGREDIENTS

Thai and Chinese cooking is amongst the world's greatest. In both, the basic philosophy of balance is the same, where the freshest produce is combined with the flavours of dried, salted and fermented ingredients, preserves and condiments. Most ingredients are now available in ordinary supermarkets and a few of the more unusual ones in Asian or Chinese groceries and markets.

AUBERGINES

Chinese aubergines are thinner with a more delicate flavour than the Mediterranean variety. They are used in many savoury dishes and in Thailand, some varieties are eaten raw with a dip or sauce.

BABY SWEETCORN

These tiny, tender cobs of sweetcorn, about 7.5 cm/3 inches long, add a crunchy texture and sweet flavour to many dishes. When buying, make sure that they are bright yellow with no brown patches, firm and crisp.

BAMBOO SHOOTS

Bamboo shoots are young, creamy-coloured, conical-shaped shoots of edible bamboo plants. They add a crunchy texture and clean, mild flavour to many dishes and are sometimes available in Chinese groceries, as well as vacuum-packed or canned in most supermarkets. If you buy the latter, transfer them to a container of water once the can has been opened. If you change the water daily, they will keep for up to five days in the refrigerator.

BASIL

Holy basil with small, dark leaves and purple stalks is frequently used in Thai cooking, although sweet basil, more easily obtainable here, may be used instead.

BEANSPROUTS

These are the shoots of the mung bean and are readily available prepacked in the vegetable section of most supermarkets. They add a wonderfully crisp texture when added to stir-fries and take only a minute or two to cook. Ideally, the brown root should be removed from each sprout and discarded, however, this is time consuming, but improves the appearance of the dish.

BLACK BEANS

These small, black soya beans may also be known as salted black beans, as they have been fermented with salt and spices. Sold loose in Chinese groceries, but also available canned, they have a rich flavour and are often used with ginger and garlic with which they have a particular affinity.

BOK CHOI

Also known as pak choi, the most common variety has long, slightly ridged white stems like celery and large, oval thick dark green leaves. Bok choi has a mild, fresh, slightly peppery taste and needs very little cooking. Choose smaller ones if possible, as they are more tender. Store in the bottom of the refrigerator.

CHILLIES

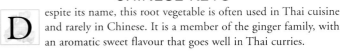

There are many different kinds of chillies and generally, the smaller they are the more fierce the heat. Red chillies are generally milder than green ones because they sweeten as they become riper. The tiny, slender tapering red or green Thai chillies are very hot and pungent. Thai cooks often include the seeds in cooking, but to moderate the heat, scrape out and discard the seeds.

CHINESE CELERY

Unlike the Western variety, Chinese celery stalks are thin, hollow and very crisp and range from pure white to dark green. Used as both a herb and a vegetable, Chinese celery is often stir-fried or used in soups and braised dishes.

CHINESE KALE

This green vegetable is popular in Thai cuisine. It has an almost earthy and slightly bitter taste and is usually served blanched and accompanied by oyster sauce. When buying, look for firm stems and fresh, dark green leaves. Store in the bottom drawer of the refrigerator for up to four days.

CHINESE KEYS

Despite its name, this root vegetable is often used in Thai cuisine and rarely in Chinese. It is a member of the ginger family, with an aromatic sweet flavour that goes well in Thai curries.

CHINESE LEAVES

Also known as Chinese cabbage, Chinese leaves look like a large, tightly packed lettuce with crinkly, pale green leaves. It adds a crunchy texture to stir-fries.

CHINESE MUSTARD CABBAGE

Also known as *gaai choi*, these mustard plants are similar in appearance to cabbages. The whole leaf is eaten, usually shredded into soups and stir-fries to which they add a fresh astringent flavour.

CORIANDER

Fresh coriander is the most popular fresh herb used in Thai cooking. It has an appearance similar to flat-leaf parsley, but has a pungent, slightly citrus flavour. Leaves, stems and roots are all used, so buy in big fresh bunches if possible.

DURIAN

This large, spiky-skinned tropical fruit has such an unpleasantly strong aroma that it is banned from public transport and hotels in Bangkok. It is expensive to buy a whole fruit, but you can sometimes buy frozen packs of skinless pieces of fruit.

GALANGAL

This is a rhizome, called *laos* or *ka* in Thailand. It is similar to ginger, but the skin is a pinkish colour and the flavour more complex and mellow. Peel it thinly and slice or grate the flesh. When sliced, it can be kept in an airtight container in the refrigerator for up to two weeks. If unavailable, ginger is an acceptable substitute.

GARLIC

This popular seasoning flavours almost all Thai and many Chinese dishes. In Thailand, garlic heads are smaller and thinner skinned, so they are often used whole as well as finely chopped or crushed. Choose firm garlic, preferably with a pinkish tinge and store in a cool, dry place, but not in the refrigerator.

GINGER

Fresh root ginger has a pungent, spicy, fresh taste. It is usually peeled, then finely chopped or grated – vary the amount of ginger used to suit your own taste. For just a hint, slice thickly and add to the dish when cooking, then remove just before serving. Fresh ginger is infinitely preferable to the powdered variety, which loses its flavour rapidly. Fresh ginger should feel firm when you buy it. If you have more than you need it can be used within a week. Store it in the freezer as it can be grated from frozen.

KAFFIR LIME LEAVES

Dark green, smooth, glossy leaves, these come from the kaffir lime tree and are highly sought after for Thai cooking. They add a distinctive citrus flavour to curries, soups and sauces. Buy them from larger supermarkets and Oriental grocery shops and keep them in a sealed polythene bag in the freezer. Lime zest can be used as an alternative.

KRACHAI

Also known as lesser ginger, this is smaller and more spicy than either ginger or galangal. It can be bought fresh in Oriental food shops or dried in small packets.

LEMON GRASS

These look a bit like spring onions, but are much tougher. The stems should be bashed to release the lemony flavour during cooking, then removed before serving. Alternatively, peel away the outer layers and chop the heart very finely.

LOTUS ROOT

This is the underwater rhizome of the lotus flower and has a lacy appearance when sliced and a sweet, crunchy flavour. Fresh lotus root takes about two hours to cook, so it is worth considering using canned lotus root instead.

MANGETOUT

These tender green pea pods with flat, barely formed peas have a deliciously crisp texture. To prepare them for cooking, simply top and tail, pulling away any string from the edges.

MOOLI

Also known as *daikon* or white radish, these look like smooth, white parsnips (they come from the same family as the radish). They have a peppery, fresh taste and are often used in salads, peeled and thinly sliced or grated. They can also be cooked, but because they have a high water content, they should be salted to extract some of the liquid, then rinsed well and steamed or boiled. They are often carved into beautiful and intricate shapes as a table decoration or garnish.

MUSHROOMS

Oyster mushrooms with their subtle flavour and delicate, almost slippery texture often feature in Chinese cooking. Now cultivated, they are widely available. The colour of the fan-shaped cap gives the mushroom its name, although they can also be pink or yellow as well as grey. Tear into long triangular segments, following the lines of the gills, and cook the smaller ones whole.

Shiitake mushrooms were originally Oriental, but they are now grown all over the world. They are more often used dried in Chinese cooking, but may also be used fresh – the caps have a strong flavour and are generally sliced and the stalks discarded. Cook the mushrooms gently for a short time, as they may toughen if overcooked. Straw mushrooms are sometimes known as double mushrooms because that is exactly what they look like; two mushrooms that grow end to end. They are small and pale brown with a pale-coloured stem.

PAPAYA

Also called pawpaw, the unripe green flesh of this tropical fruit is often used in Thai cooking. It ripens to a deep orange colour and is delicious sliced and served as a dessert.

SHALLOTS

Small, mild-flavoured members of the onion family, shallots have coppery-coloured skins. Use them in the same way as onions, or thinly slice and deep-fry to use as a garnish.

SPRING ONIONS

Long, slender spring onions are the immature bulbs of yellow onions. They are frequently used in stir fries, as they cook within minutes.

TAMARIND

This adds an essential sour taste to many dishes. It is extracted from the pods as a sticky brown pulp, which is soaked to make tamarind water.

TOFU

Tofu or bean curd has been used as an ingredient in Thai and Chinese cooking for over 1000 years. Made from yellow soya beans, which are soaked, ground and briefly cooked, tofu is very rich in protein and low in calories. Because of its bland taste it is ideal cooked with stronger flavourings. It is usually available in two types: a soft variety known as silken tofu that can be used for soups and desserts, and a firm, solid white block, which can be cubed or sliced and included in stir-frying and braising. Also available is smoked tofu, which is a seasoned bean curd. When using, cut into the required size with care and do not stir too much when cooking; it simply needs to be heated through.

WATER CHESTNUTS

These are bulbs of an Asian water plant that look like and are a similar size to chestnuts. When peeled, the inner flesh is very crisp. Some Oriental grocers sell them fresh, although canned, either whole or sliced, are almost as good.

WATER SPINACH

This is widely grown throughout Asia and is unrelated to ordinary spinach. The leaves are elongated and tender and the stems fine and delicate. Water spinach requires minimal cooking. It is cooked in the same way as spinach, either steamed, stir-fried or added to soups.

YARD-LONG BEANS

Although unrelated to French beans, they are similar in appearance, but about four times longer. As they grow, they start to curl and are often sold in looped bunches. Two varieties exist: a pale green type and a much darker, thinner variety. They are very popular and may be found in great quantities in Chinese markets. The Cantonese often cook them with black beans or fermented bean curd and in Sichuan, they are deep-fried. Store in a plastic bag in the refrigerator for up to four days. To prepare, cut into lengths and use in exactly the same way as French beans.

DRY, CANNED AND PRESERVED INGREDIENTS

BIRD'S NEST

This is literally a bird's nest made from the spittle of a swallow and can occasionally be found in Chinese food shops. It is sold as a crunchy jelly that is often added to sauces, soups and extravagant stuffings and is an acquired taste. Since it is dried, it can be stored in a dry place for several years. To use, it should be soaked overnight in cold water, then simmered for 20 minutes in fresh water.

CASHEW NUTS

These milky-flavoured nuts with a crunchy texture, are often used whole or chopped in Chinese cooking, particularly as an ingredient in chicken dishes.

CASSIA

This is the bark taken from a cassia or laurel tree and is dark brown and flat in shape. It is similar, but slightly less subtle than cinnamon.

CHILLIES

Dried red chillies are used throughout Thailand and in many regions of China. The drying process concentrates the flavour, making them more fiery. Look for dried chillies with a bright red colour and a pungent aroma. If stored in a sealed container, they will keep almost indefinitely. Chilli oil is made from crushed dried chillies or whole fresh chillies and is used as both a seasoning and a dipping condiment. Chilli powder is made from dried red chillies and is usually mixed with other spices and seasonings, ranging from mild and aromatic to very hot – always check the jar before using. Chilli bean sauce is a thick, dark paste made from soya beans, chillies and other spicy seasonings and is very hot. Seal the jar after use and store in the refrigerator.

COCONUT MILK

Rich, creamy coconut milk is extracted from the white flesh of the nut. It can be bought in cans or made by adding boiling water to a sachet of coconut powder. Sometimes an opaque, white cream rises to the top of canned coconut milk and solidifies. You should shake the can before opening. If the milk is stored in an airtight container in the refrigerator it will last for up to three days, however, it does not freeze well. Occasionally, freshly made coconut milk may be bought from Oriental groceries. It is often used in Thai cooking, especially in curries and may also be used in desserts.

CORIANDER

Ground coriander is made from coriander seeds and has an almost sweet, spicy, fresh flavour. You can buy it ready ground or instead toast whole seeds in the oven and grind them yourself.

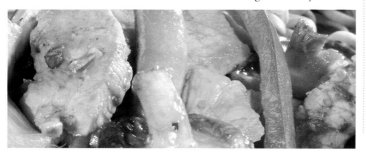

CREAMED COCONUT

Made from coconut oils and other fats, this comes in a hard, white block. It is not a substitute for coconut milk and is usually added at the end of cooking, to thicken a sauce, or to add coconut flavour to a finished dish.

GROUNDNUT OIL

Also known as peanut oil, this has a mild, nutty flavour. Because it can be heated to high temperatures, it is ideal for both stir-frying and deep-frying.

HOISIN SAUCE

This is a thick, dark brownish-red sauce, which is sweet, tangy and spicy. Made from soya beans, salt, flour, sugar, vinegar, chilli, garlic and sesame oil, it may be used as a dip, in 'red-cooking' and as a baste for roasted meats.

MUSHROOMS

Many sorts of dried mushrooms are used in Thai and Chinese cooking. Cloud ear (black fungus) mushrooms need soaking in warm water for about 20 minutes before use. They have a subtle, mild flavour and are highly regarded for their colour and gelatinous flavour. Dried shiitake mushrooms have a very strong flavour and are used in small quantities. After soaking, the hard stalks are usually discarded or added to stock.

NAM PLA FISH SAUCE

This is a golden brown, thin sauce with a salty flavour and is made from salted and fermented fresh fish, usually anchovies. It is used in Thai cooking in much the same way as soy sauce is used in Chinese cooking. The fishy aroma is almost unpleasant when the bottle is opened, but this mellows when mixed with other ingredients, adding a unique Thai flavour.

NOODLES

There are many types of noodles used in Thai and Chinese cuisine. The most popular include: cellophane noodles – also known as glass noodles – that are white and become transparent when cooked. Made from ground mung beans, they are never served on their own, but are added to soups or are deep-fried and used as a garnish. Egg noodles can be bought fresh, but the dried ones, which come in fine and medium, are just as good. Generally, flat noodles are used in soups and round ones for stir-fries. Rice noodles are fine, opaque noodles made from rice flour and are also called rice sticks. They are common in southern China, as it is the rice growing area of the country. Wheat is the primary grain in northern China and is made into noodles without egg. These noodles are sold in compressed square packages and bundles. *Yifu* noodles are round, yellow noodles, woven in a round cake and are often sold precooked.

OYSTER SAUCE

This is a thick, brown sauce made from oysters cooked in soy sauce. It has a wonderfully rich, but not fishy flavour, as this disappears during processing. Often used as a condiment, it is also one of the most used ingredients in southern Chinese cuisine.

PLUM SAUCE

 s the name suggests, plum sauce is made from plums that are simmered together with vinegar, sugar, ginger, chilli and other spices.

RICE

 lutinous rice is a short-grain variety often used in desserts. It is sometimes referred to as sticky rice. Thai Jasmine rice is a long-grain rice from Thailand with an aromatic and subtle flavour.

RICE PAPER

his is made from a mixture of rice flour, water and salt, which is rolled out by machine until it is paper-thin and dried. It comes in round or triangular pieces which can be softened by placing between two damp tea towels and are then used to make spring rolls.

RICE VINEGARS

here are several varieties: white vinegar is clear and mild; red vinegar is slightly sweet and quite salty and is often used as a dipping sauce; black vinegar is very rich, yet mild and sweet vinegar is very thick, dark-coloured and flavoured with star anise.

RICE WINE

ften used in Chinese cooking in both marinades and sauces, rice wine is made from glutinous rice and has a rich, mellow taste. Do not confuse rice wine with sake, which is the Japanese version, as it is very different. Pale dry sherry is a good substitute for rice wine.

SESAME OIL

his is a thick, dark-golden to brown aromatic oil that is made from sesame seeds. It is rarely used in frying, as it has a low smoke-point, but when it is, it should be combined with another oil. It is often added to a finished dish in small quantities.

SESAME PASTE

esame paste is a rich, very creamy brown paste made from sesame seeds, however, it is not the same as tahini paste from the Middle-East. If unavailable, use smooth peanut butter, which has a similar texture.

SESAME SEEDS

hese are the dried seeds of the sesame herb. Unhulled, the seeds may be dull white to black in colour, but once the hull is removed, the seeds are a creamy-white colour. Sesame seeds are often used as a garnish or as a light coating to add crunch to food. Toast them first, to intensify their flavour, by shaking over heat in a dry frying pan until the seeds are lightly coloured.

SHRIMP PASTE

 ade from puréed, fermented salted shrimps, this is popular in Thai cooking and adds a distinctive fishy flavour. There is also a Chinese version, which has an even stronger aroma. Use both sparingly. Dried salted shrimps are also available, which are sometimes used as a seasoning in stir-fries. They should be soaked first in warm water, then puréed in a blender or made into a paste with a pestle and mortar.

SOY SAUCE

oth light and dark soy sauce feature frequently in Chinese and Thai cooking. It is made from a mixture of soya beans, flour and water that are fermented together and allowed to age. The resulting liquid which is then distilled is soy sauce. Light soy sauce has a lighter colour and is more salty than the dark variety. It is often labelled as 'superior soy'. Dark soy sauce is aged for longer and the colour is almost black. Its flavour is stronger and is slightly thicker than light soy sauce. Confusingly, this is labelled in Thai and Chinese food shops as 'Soy Superior Sauce'. It is also possible to buy a mushroom soy sauce, which is made by the infusion of dry straw mushrooms and a shrimp-flavoured soy sauce.

STAR ANISE

 his is an eight-pointed, star-shaped pod with a strong aniseed flavour. It is added whole to many Chinese dishes, but is usually removed before serving. It is also a vital ingredient in Chinese five spice powder.

SUGAR

dded in small quantities to many savoury Thai dishes, sugar balances the flavour of a dish, and gives a shiny appearance to the sauces. Thai palm sugar comes in large lumps or slabs, which need to be bashed with a mallet, to break into smaller pieces. Brown coffee crystals make a good alternative.

SZECHUAN PEPPERCORNS

his small reddish spice has a distinct, woody flavour and is more fragrantly spicy than hot. It is one of the spices in Chinese five spice powder. Also known as *fargara* and Chinese pepper, Szechuan peppercorns are used extensively in Sichuan cooking. Unrelated to peppers, they are the dried berries of a shrub and have a slight numbing effect on the tongue.

THAI CURRY PASTE

ed curry paste is a strongly flavoured spicy paste made mainly from dried red chillies that are blended with other spices and herbs. There is also green curry paste, which is hotter and made from fresh green chillies.

THOUSAND-YEAR-OLD EGGS

resh duck eggs are often preserved in brine, which seeps into the shell, making the whites salty and the yolks firm and orange-coloured. Thousand-year-old eggs are preserved in a mixture of clay, fine ash and salt. The whites of the eggs turn a translucent black and the yolks a grey-green colour after a year or so, hence their name. Unopened eggs can be kept for many months.

TURMERIC

his mild flavoured spice adds a bright yellow hue to foods. Although it can sometimes be bought fresh, it is most often used in its dried powdered form. Wonton wrappers, also called wonton skins, are egg and flour pastry-like wrappings that can be stuffed then fried, steamed or added to soups. Fresh ones may be stored for about five days in the refrigerator if kept wrapped in clingfilm.

YELLOW BEAN SAUCE

 his thick, aromatic sauce is made with fermented yellow beans, flour and salt and adds a distinctive flavour to sauces.

EQUIPMENT

There is little equipment that is absolutely essential to preparing and cooking Thai and Chinese food, but many tools will make the task easier and give more authentic results.

BAMBOO STRAINER This is a wide, flat, metal strainer with a bamboo handle. It makes removing cooked food from hot oil or water much easier. Of course, an ordinary metal slotted spoon may be used instead.

CHOPSTICKS Food is usually eaten with chopsticks in China, but in Thailand they are rarely used and a spoon and fork is much more usual. Wooden chopsticks are inexpensive, but plastic ones are more hygienic and can be reused many times.

CLEAVERS are used to slice, chop, shred, fillet, dice and crush. It is such an all-purpose tool that skilled Thai and Chinese cooks need no other knives, although they may have several weights (light, medium and heavy) of cleaver. The best quality are made with tempered carbon steel, so that the blade can be kept razor sharp, although a good-quality stainless steel one is less likely to rust.

ELECTRIC RICE COOKER Since many meals are accompanied by rice, most modern Thai and Chinese kitchens have an electric rice cooker. It is the easiest way to cook rice to perfection with little attention.

SPATULA A long-handled spatula with a shovel-shaped end for stir-frying food is relatively inexpensive, although you can use a long-handled wooden spoon if you prefer.

STEAMERS You can either use a stainless steel steamer, with small round perforations, that fits over a saucepan or buy a more traditional bamboo steamer. You will need one or more tiers plus a lid to fit. It is a good idea to briefly wash the bamboo steamer before using it for the first time and to steam it while empty for a few minutes.

WOK This is probably the most useful and versatile piece of equipment and is used for stir-frying, deep-frying and steaming. The traditional shape has deep, sloping sides and a rounded base to ensure quick, even cooking. In stir-frying, it is possible to move the food around without pieces spilling over the edges and in deep-frying the rounded shape means that considerably less oil is needed than in a conventional pan. This shape is, however, only suitable for use on a gas hob and if yours is electric, you will need a wok with a flatter base that is specifically designed for use on electric hobs.

There are two basic types of wok: the Cantonese version, which has small handles on either side, which may be wooden or metal and the *pau* or Peking wok which has a long handle. When choosing a wok, make sure it is large enough for your needs; most are about 30.5–3.5 cm/12–14 inches in diameter, but some are much smaller. Even if you only cook for one or two people, most of the time a large wok is still preferable. Pick a heavier wok, but remember you will need to be able to lift it when full of food. Those made of carbon steel can take very high heat without scorching the food. Nonstick versions are now available, which means that you can reduce the fat in many recipes. Nonstick woks are also useful when adding ingredients with a high acid level such as vinegar.

Wok accessories include domed lids, metal racks and metal frames. Domed lids are usually made from light aluminium and are vital for steaming and keeping food hot. A metal rack can easily be clipped on to the edge of the wok making it useful for draining or reserving food. You will also need a wok stand – a metal frame that holds the wok firm and sufficiently far enough away from the heat. For safety, always make sure this is securely in place before setting your wok on it and starting to cook.

Before use, all woks, unless nonstick should be seasoned. First give the wok a good wash in very hot, soapy water. This will remove the protective coat of oil applied by the manufacturer to prevent the wok from being marked by the packaging or damaged during transit. Pour 1 tablespoon of groundnut or corn oil into the wok and rub it all over the inside with absorbent kitchen paper. Gently heat the wok for about 5 minutes, then wipe it clean, If the absorbent kitchen paper is black, you should repeat this process. With age, your wok will darken; this is normal and you should not scour it to remove this colouring. Always make sure that you dry the wok thoroughly before putting it away to prevent rusting.

COOKING TECHNIQUES

DEEP-FRYING When deep-frying in a wok, pour in enough oil to come no more than halfway up the wok. Gently heat until the required temperature is reached, preferably using a cooking thermometer. Alternatively, you can test the temperature by dropping in a small cube of bread; bubbles should quickly form all over the surface. Carefully add the food to the oil with tongs or a slotted spoon and move it around occasionally while cooking to keep the pieces separate. It is far better to cook in batches than to add all the food at once, as you may risk the oil bubbling up too much and the temperature of the oil to drop, making the outside soggy. Remove the food when cooked and drain on absorbent kitchen paper to soak up any excess oil, before serving. Always make sure that the wok is secure before you start cooking and never leave it unattended. A deep-fat fryer is a costly, but useful piece of equipment if you deep-fry foods often and you may find it safer and easier to use than a wok.

STEAMING This is a gentle and moist method of cooking, especially good for delicate foods such as fish. It relies on the heat circulating around the food, so make sure you leave a little space between each item, when adding. After arranging, place the steamer above simmering water in a wok or saucepan. To prevent any food sticking to the steamer, you can line it first with a piece of muslin. If liked, add a few slices of fresh ginger to the water and a bay leaf. This not only adds a slight flavouring to the food, but makes a wonderful aroma in the kitchen and can help mask cooking smells especially if you are steaming fish. Steam for the recommended time and check the water level in the pan or wok occasionally, topping up with more boiling water if necessary. If you do not have a steamer you can use a wok instead. Place a trivet in the wok and pour in enough boiling water to come to just below the level of the trivet. Place the food to be steamed on a heatproof plate and put on top of the trivet. Cover and steam as before.

STIR-FRYING This quick-cook technique retains the fresh flavour, colour and texture of food. It is essential to have all ingredients prepared before you start cooking. Heat the wok for about a minute over a high heat, then add the oil and swirl it around to coat the base and about halfway up the sides. Continue heating until hot but not smoking, so that when the food is added it starts to cook straight away. Add the ingredients, one at a time, tossing and stirring continuously. Aromatics such as garlic and ginger are usually added first, followed by the main ingredients that need longer cooking such as meat and finally those that need little cooking or only a brief heating through. Liquids and sauces are usually added towards the end of cooking and then bubbled for a minute or two.

SPICE MIXTURES AND FLAVOURINGS Although these can be bought, by making your own basic seasoning mixtures, your finished dishes will have an unmistakable fresh flavour – adjust the spices to suit your individual taste.

CRISPY BASIL This makes an attractive garnish sprinkled over savoury dishes. Use holy (Thai) basil if you can find it, although sweet Italian basil works just as well. Take 25 g/1 oz fresh basil leaves and 1 deseeded and finely sliced red chilli. Heat 3 tablespoons of groundnut oil in a wok until very hot, add the basil and chilli and stir-fry for 1–2 minutes or until crispy. Remove with a slotted spoon and drain on absorbent kitchen paper.

CRISPY SEAWEED This is often used as a garnish on Chinese dishes and is made in exactly the same way. Finely shred a piece of dark green cabbage – a Savoy is ideal – and deep-fry in groundnut oil at 180°C/350°F for about 1 minute until crispy. Sprinkle with a little finely ground sea salt and scatter over the dish or serve separately as a side dish.

FRESH COCONUT MILK Take a fresh coconut, push a large skewer into the three holes at the top and drain out the liquid. Put the coconut in a thick plastic bag and hit it hard with a hammer to break. Remove the outer shell from the pieces of coconut flesh by prising off with a sharp knife, then peel away the thin brown skin. Coarsely grate the flesh, put in a food processor and blend until very fine. Pour in 300 ml/½ pint of boiling water, briefly process, then leave for 15 minutes. Strain the mixture through a sieve lined with muslin. When drained, draw the corners of the muslin together and squeeze out the last drops of liquid. Repeat the process with the coconut and a further 300 ml/½ pint of boiling water and add to the first batch of coconut milk. Store in the refrigerator for up to 48 hours, but do not freeze. A solid, fatty cream may rise to the top, so give it a good stir before using.

You can also make coconut milk from desiccated coconut. Put 350 g/12 oz in a saucepan with 300 ml/½ pint water and simmer for 3–4 minutes. Briefly blend in a food processor, then make in the same way as fresh coconut milk, adding a second lot of boiling water to the squeezed-dry coconut.

GREEN CURRY PASTE Roughly chop 6 spring onions, 1 lemon grass stalk, 2 peeled garlic cloves, 8 fresh green chillies (remove the seeds if you want a milder paste), 2.5 cm/1 inch piece of fresh root ginger and 25 g/1 oz fresh coriander leaves, stalks and roots. Remove and discard the central vein from 2 kaffir lime leaves and finely shred. Put all the ingredients in a food processor with 2 tablespoons of groundnut oil and a pinch of salt. Blend to a paste, then transfer to a jar and store for up to three weeks in the refrigerator.

RED CURRY PASTE Remove the seeds from 8 fresh red chillies and roughly chop. Put in a food processor with 2.5 cm/1 inch piece fresh root ginger, 2 peeled shallots, 1 lemon grass stalk and 4 peeled garlic cloves, all roughly chopped. Add 2 teaspoons of coriander seeds, 1 teaspoon of cumin seeds and 1 teaspoon of hot paprika, a pinch of turmeric and salt, 1 tablespoon of lime juice and 2 tablespoons of groundnut oil. Blend to a paste, transfer to a jar and store for up to three weeks in the refrigerator.

CUSTOMS AND TRADITIONS

Chinese and Thai food has become increasingly popular in this country during recent years. There are many similarities between the two cuisines, yet their history, climate and culture has created subtle differences between them.

CHINESE CUISINE

Although China is a vast country, the basic principles of cooking is remarkably similar throughout the regions. Economical fuel-saving methods of cooking have developed over the years, such as fast and furious stir-frying, where food is cut up into small, even-sized pieces so it cooks in very little time; steaming where baskets are stacked layer upon layer; and slow simmering in a large pot to make use of the last remaining embers of the fire. Few things go to waste in the Chinese kitchen and some of their greatest delicacies have been created from scraps that Westerners would simply throw away.

Chinese cuisine falls into four main culinary regions: Cantonese or Southern, Peking or Northern, North China and Shanghai or Eastern. Peking cuisine is famous for seafood, pork and sweet-and-sour dishes, as well as more unusual ingredients like bird's nest and shark's fin. In Chinese the word *fan* means both rice and meal and rice accompanies almost every meal in the South. Long-grain rice is the most commonly used, but Thai jasmine rice is served on special occasions, as is sticky or glutinous rice which is also used for desserts.

Peking or Northern cuisine is associated with a refined style of cooking, since many classical dishes have been handed down from the Imperial kitchen. Here there is a notable use of lamb, garlic, spring onions and leeks. Food tends to be sweet and sour, but with much more emphasis on the sour rather than sweet. North China is an area where wheat rather than rice is grown and wheat-based noodles are popular. In Shanghai or Eastern China vegetables and rice are plentiful and it is here that rice wine and vinegar are made. Many dishes from this region have a sweet flavour as sugar is commonly used as a seasoning. Szechuan or Western cuisine is very fiery and spicy, where chillies and Sichuan pepper feature in virtually every savoury dish.

THE CHINESE MEAL

In China, dishes are served all together and not in separate courses. The Chinese rarely eat on their own and enjoy sharing a meal, dining with family or a group of friends. Rice is served in individual dishes, topped with a portion from a central meat or vegetable dish. When this has been eaten, each person helps himself to another dish, transferring it to their plate using chopsticks (which should never touch the lips).

Many dishes have descriptive and romantic names, such as Five Flower Pork for belly pork, named after the five layers of skin, fat, lean, fat and lean. Certain numbers are considered lucky, so often dishes are given names such as Eight Treasures, even though there may not be eight ingredients! Phoenix and dragon are the terms sometimes used for prawns and chicken.

In Szechuan, chillies, fermented bean paste and sesame oil are used in varying combinations to produce dishes with evocative names including Strange Taste (*Guai Wei*), Familiar Taste (*Jiachanh Wei*) and Peppery Taste (*Xiangla Wei*). Drinks are not usually drunk with the meal, but a bowl of soup is often provided to wash the food down when needed. At the end, tea may be served. Grown in China for more than 3000 years, there is a large range of teas that can be divided into three main types: Green tea, *oolong* tea and black tea. Green tea is unfermented and a pale fragrant drink without milk or sugar. Among green teas is gunpowder, named by the British because the tea resembled lead shot and Jasmine tea, which is flavoured with dried jasmine petals. *Oolong* tea is semi-fermented, with a stronger flavour, but is not as strong as black tea, which is fully fermented and has a hint of sweetness. Black teas include, *keemum* (which has a slightly nutty flavour) and *Lapsang Souchong*.

Although the Chinese have an incredibly sweet tooth and enjoy puddings and cakes, these are not served at the end of the meal, as in the West. They are eaten, instead, at formal banquets where they are served part way though the meal.

CELEBRATIONS

Chinese New Year is probably the best known celebration and is a time of reunion and thanksgiving. It is a religious ceremony in honour of Heaven and Earth, the gods of the household and family ancestors. The head of each household offers incense, flowers, food and wine to ensure good fortune in the coming year. On New Year's Eve a banquet is held called *weilu* meaning 'surrounding the stove', which celebrates both present and past generations. Every dish served has a name, which symbolises either honour, health or wealth. A soup, for example, may be called Broth of Prosperity and strands of vermicelli referred to as 'silvery threads of longevity'.

After the feast, parents give their children small red envelopes that contain 'lucky' money. In the next few days, friends and relatives visit and more meals must be prepared. Snacks and sweetmeats are offered before the main dishes such as pomegranate seeds, candied lotus root and almonds, all representing fertility and long life.

At the heart of many Chinese celebrations is the principle of balance and harmony. The beginning of each new season is important, as are the Buddhist and Taoist principles of *yin* and *yang* (female and male). Cooking ingredients are mixed and matched in the same way; sweet and sour, or hot and sour, for example. On birthday meals, noodles are usually served to represent long life. For luck, they should always be eaten whole and not broken into pieces. Dim Sum, meaning 'heart's delight' are popular Chinese snacks. These dumplings are filled with either vegetables or spiced meat and are often deep-fried or steamed. They are traditionally eaten with tea for breakfast, lunch or sold on the street to be eaten between meals. They play an important part during most festivals, including Chinese New Year when they are eaten in place of normal meals.

THAI CUISINE

Thai food has been influenced by many countries, notably India, Burma and especially China. Yet, the Thais have refined these to a unique cuisine of their own, characterised by the contrasting flavours of sharp citrus lime leaves and lemon grass, hot chillies, ginger and galangal and sour tamarind, often brought together and mellowed by creamy coconut milk. Thai cuisine is similar to Chinese in that rice is a staple food (the Thai words used when inviting guests are 'come and have rice with us'), together with plenty of fresh vegetables and only small amounts of meat. Dairy products are used very little, and for both religious and climatic reasons, red meats such as beef feature in few dishes.

As in Chinese cooking, food has a subtle balance of sweet, sour and salty. Fish has always been important in the Thai diet as the entire country is crossed by rivers and there is miles of coastline, where freshwater fish and shellfish are plentiful. Flooded rice fields sustain ducks, frogs, eels and yet more fish. Much of this is dried, salted or made into fermented sauces and pastes, which add a distinctive flavour to many dishes. Thailand is an extremely fertile land with a tropical climate and cooler central highlands where an abundance of different ingredients are found. The Thais produce some of the finest foods in the world and it is the only country in Asia to export more food than it imports.

The Thais are passionate about food. Shopping for food is as much of a skill as cooking it. Street markets are very much a way of life; everything arrives fresh in the morning and by mid-afternoon almost everything has been sold.

THE THAI MEAL

A Thai meal is all about sharing. It generally consists of a number of different dishes, plus a huge bowl of rice. Sometimes there is a soup or a curry, some noodles and fresh fruit such as *rambutans*, *mangosteens* and *durians*. All these dishes come to the table at the same time, so everyone has the chance to help themselves to a little of each. Just as in China, a large pile of rice on individual plates will be topped with one or two portions of the dishes. When these are finished, other dishes will be sampled.

Food is eaten with either a spoon and fork or with fingers, although noodles are eaten with chopsticks. A knife is not needed, because all the food has been cut up before cooking. Desserts are only served on special occasions and generally a meal will be finished with fruit.

In the recipes in this book and when eating out in Thai restaurants, you may come across some of these terms.

GAENG This is a curry that is often quite hot, including *Gaeng Ped Red Curry* and *Gaeng Phanaeng*, which is a dry curry that has a thicker, milder sauce.

GAENG CHUD This is a soup and one of the best known is *Tom Yam Kung*, which is made with prawns. Another popular soup is *Tom Khaa Gai*, which is made with chicken, galangal and coconut milk.

KHANOM This is a sweetened dish, although it may be a savoury food and often consists of small individual items served in banana leaf parcels.

MEE OR SEN These are noodles that may be made from rice, wheat or mung beans. *Kuiteow* are large fresh noodles and are usually fried with vegetables. *Mee Krob* are wheat noodles that are deep-fried, coated with a sugar syrup and served as a savoury.

CELEBRATIONS

Most important occasions in Thailand have a religious element and before the adaptation of the European Sunday, working days were broken up by holy days. April 6th is *Chakri* day when the founding of the present dynasty is celebrated and flowers are taken to the temple of the Emerald Buddha. The King's birthday, the anniversary of his coronation and the Queen's birthday are all national holidays and are celebrated with parades and fireworks. Elaborate banquets have a great part to play in the celebrations and presentation is very important where food is exquisitely garnished with carved fruit and vegetables. The two greatest events in any Thai life are when a son becomes a monk for a short time (as most Thai males do) and weddings, which are still regarded as the union of two families, rather than individuals. At weddings the Thai sweet *Look Choob* is served, once only eaten by the Kings of Thailand. This is made from a soya bean paste blended with sugar and coconut juice and shaped into tiny fruit and vegetables. The importance of the family can be seen in the Thai approach to dining, whether at a simple meal at home or in a smart restaurant.

CLEAR CHICKEN & MUSHROOM SOUP

INGREDIENTS   Serves 4

2 large chicken legs, about
  450 g/1 lb total weight
1 tbsp groundnut oil
1 tsp sesame oil
1 onion, peeled and very
  thinly sliced
2.5 cm/1 inch piece root
  ginger, peeled and very
  finely chopped
1.1 litres/2 pints clear chicken
  stock

1 lemon grass stalk, bruised
50 g/2 oz long-grain rice
75 g/3 oz button mushrooms,
  wiped and finely sliced
4 spring onions, trimmed, cut
  into 5 cm/2 inch pieces and
  shredded
1 tbsp dark soy sauce
4 tbsp dry sherry
salt and freshly ground black
  pepper

1 Skin the chicken legs and remove any fat. Cut each in half to make 2 thigh and 2 drumstick portions and reserve. Heat the groundnut and sesame oils in a large saucepan. Add the sliced onion and cook gently for 10 minutes, or until soft but not beginning to colour.

2 Add the chopped ginger to the saucepan and cook for about 30 seconds, stirring all the time to prevent it sticking, then pour in the stock. Add the chicken pieces and the lemon grass, cover and simmer gently for 15 minutes. Stir in the rice and cook for a further 15 minutes or until the chicken is cooked.

3 Remove the chicken from the saucepan and leave until cool enough to handle. Finely shred the flesh, then return to the saucepan with the mushrooms, spring onions, soy sauce and sherry. Simmer for 5 minutes, or until the rice and mushrooms are tender. Remove the lemon grass.

4 Season the soup to taste with salt and pepper. Ladle into warmed serving bowls, making sure each has an equal amount of shredded chicken and vegetables and serve immediately.

FOOD FACT

Tahini is a thick paste made from sesame seeds. It is available from many delicatessens and super-markets as well as Oriental food stores. It is most often used in making hummus.

CREAMY CHICKEN & TOFU SOUP

INGREDIENTS

Serves 4–6

225 g/8 oz firm tofu, drained
3 tbsp groundnut oil
1 garlic clove, peeled and
   crushed
2.5 cm/1 inch piece root ginger,
   peeled and finely chopped
2.5 cm/1 inch piece fresh
   galangal, peeled and finely
   sliced (if available)
1 lemon grass stalk, bruised
¼ tsp ground turmeric
600 ml/1 pint chicken stock

600 ml/1 pint coconut milk
225 g/8 oz cauliflower, cut into
   tiny florets
1 medium carrot, peeled and
   cut into thin matchsticks
125 g/4 oz green beans,
   trimmed and cut in half
75 g/3 oz thin egg noodles
225 g/8 oz cooked chicken,
   shredded
salt and freshly ground black
   pepper

1 Cut the tofu into 1 cm/
½ inch cubes, then pat dry
on absorbent kitchen paper.

2 Heat 1 tablespoon of the
oil in a nonstick frying pan.
Fry the tofu in 2 batches for 3–4
minutes or until golden brown.
Remove, drain on absorbent
kitchen paper and reserve.

3 Heat the remaining oil in
a large saucepan. Add the
garlic, ginger, galangal and lemon
grass and cook for about 30
seconds. Stir in the turmeric,
then pour in the stock and
coconut milk and bring to the
boil. Reduce the heat to a gentle
simmer, add the cauliflower
and carrots and simmer for
10 minutes. Add the green
beans and simmer for a further
5 minutes.

4 Meanwhile, bring a large
saucepan of lightly salted
water to the boil. Add the noodles,
turn off the heat, cover and leave
to cook or cook according to the
packet instructions.

5 Remove the lemon grass from
the soup. Drain the noodles and
stir into the soup with the chicken
and browned tofu. Season to taste
with salt and pepper, then simmer
gently for 2–3 minutes or until
heated through. Serve immediately
in warmed soup bowls.

FOOD FACT

Tofu is a white curd made
from soya beans. It originated
in China and is made in a
similar way to cheese.

WONTON NOODLE SOUP

INGREDIENTS

Serves 4

4 shiitake mushrooms, wiped
125 g/4 oz raw prawns, peeled and finely chopped
125 g/4 oz pork mince
4 water chestnuts, finely chopped
4 spring onions, trimmed and finely sliced
1 medium egg white

salt and freshly ground black pepper
1½ tsp cornflour
1 packet fresh wonton wrappers
1.1 litres/2 pints chicken stock
2 cm/¾ inch piece root ginger, peeled and sliced
75 g/3 oz thin egg noodles
125 g/4 oz pak choi, shredded

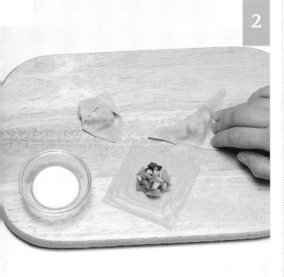

1 Place the mushrooms in a bowl, cover with warm water and leave to soak for 1 hour. Drain, remove and discard the stalks and finely chop the mushrooms. Return to the bowl with the prawns, pork, water chestnuts, 2 of the spring onions and egg white. Season to taste with salt and pepper. Mix well.

2 Mix the cornflour with 1 tablespoon of cold water to make a paste. Place a wonton wrapper on a board and brush the edges with the paste. Drop a little less than 1 teaspoon of the pork mixture in the centre then fold in half to make a triangle, pressing the edges together. Bring the 2 outer corners together, fixing together with a little more paste. Continue until all the pork mixture is used up; you should have 16–20 wontons.

3 Pour the stock into a large wide saucepan, add the ginger slices and bring to the boil. Add the wontons and simmer for about 5 minutes. Add the noodles and cook for 1 minute. Stir in the pak choi and cook for a further 2 minutes, or until the noodles and pak choi are tender and the wontons have floated to the surface and are cooked through.

4 Ladle the soup into warmed bowls, discarding the ginger. Sprinkle with the remaining sliced spring onion and serve immediately.

FOOD FACT

Wonton wrappers are thin, almost see-through sheets of dough made from eggs and flour, about 10 cm/4 inches square. Buy them fresh or frozen from larger super-markets and Oriental stores.

THAI SHELLFISH SOUP

INGREDIENTS   Serves 4–6

350 g/12 oz raw prawns
350 g/12 oz firm white fish,
  such as monkfish, cod or
  haddock
175 g/ 6 oz small squid rings
1 tbsp lime juice
450 g/1 lb live mussels
400 ml/15 fl oz coconut milk
1 tbsp groundnut oil

2 tbsp Thai red curry paste
1 lemon grass stalk, bruised
3 kaffir lime leaves, finely
  shredded
2 tbsp Thai fish sauce
salt and freshly ground black
  pepper
fresh coriander leaves, to
  garnish

1 Peel the prawns. Using a sharp knife, remove the black vein along the back of the prawns. Pat dry with absorbent kitchen paper and reserve.

2 Skin the fish, pat dry and cut into 2.5 cm/1 inch chunks. Place in a bowl with the prawns and the squid rings. Sprinkle with the lime juice and reserve.

3 Scrub the mussels, removing their beards and any barnacles. Discard any mussels that are open, damaged or that do not close when tapped. Place in a large saucepan and add 150 ml/¼ pint of coconut milk.

4 Cover, bring to the boil, then simmer for 5 minutes, or until the mussels open, shaking the saucepan occasionally. Lift out the mussels, discarding any unopened ones, strain the liquid through a muslin-lined sieve and reserve.

5 Rinse and dry the saucepan. Heat the groundnut oil, add the curry paste and cook for 1 minute, stirring all the time. Add the lemon grass, lime leaves, fish sauce and pour in both the strained and the remaining coconut milk. Bring the contents of the saucepan to a very gentle simmer.

6 Add the fish mixture to the saucepan and simmer for 2–3 minutes or until just cooked. Stir in the mussels, with or without their shells as preferrred. Season to taste with salt and pepper, then garnish with coriander leaves. Ladle into warmed bowls and serve immediately.

FOOD FACT

Sprinkling fish and seafood with lime juice improves its texture, as the acid in the juice firms up the flesh.

Moo Shi Pork

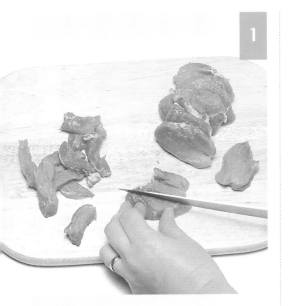

INGREDIENTS   Serves 4

175 g/6 oz pork fillet
2 tsp Chinese rice wine or dry
  sherry
2 tbsp light soy sauce
1 tsp cornflour
25 g/1 oz dried golden
  needles, soaked and drained
2 tbsp groundnut oil
3 medium eggs, lightly beaten
1 tsp freshly grated root ginger

3 spring onions, trimmed and
  thinly sliced
150 g/5 oz bamboo shoots, cut
  into fine strips
salt and freshly ground black
  pepper
8 mandarin pancakes, steamed
hoisin sauce
sprigs of fresh coriander, to
  garnish

1 Cut the pork across the grain into 1 cm/½ inch slices, then cut into thin strips. Place in a bowl with the Chinese rice wine or sherry, soy sauce and cornflour. Mix well and reserve. Trim off the tough ends of the golden needles, then cut in half and reserve.

2 Heat a wok or large frying pan, add 1 tablespoon of the groundnut oil and when hot, add the lightly beaten eggs, and cook for 1 minute, stirring all the time, until scrambled. Remove and reserve. Wipe the wok clean with absorbent kitchen paper.

3 Return the wok to the heat, add the remaining oil and when hot transfer the pork strips from the marinade mixture to the wok, shaking off as much marinade as possible. Stir-fry for 30 seconds, then add the ginger, spring onions and bamboo shoots and pour in the marinade. Stir-fry for 2–3 minutes or until cooked.

4 Return the scrambled eggs to the wok, season to taste with salt and pepper and stir for a few seconds until mixed well and heated through. Divide the mixture between the pancakes, drizzle each with 1 teaspoon of hoisin sauce and roll up. Garnish and serve immediately.

HELPFUL HINT

Golden needles, also known as tiger lily buds, are dried, unopened lily flowers. They are about 5 cm/2 inches long, have a slightly furry texture and are strongly fragrant. Buy those that are brightly golden in colour and store in a cool, dark place. They need to be soaked in hot water for about 30 minutes before use, then rinsed and squeezed dry. Omit them if you prefer and increase the quantity of pork to 225 g/8 oz.

CRISPY PORK WONTONS

INGREDIENTS   Serves 4

1 small onion, peeled and
  roughly chopped
2 garlic cloves, peeled and
  crushed
1 green chilli, deseeded and
  chopped
2.5 cm/1 inch piece fresh root
  ginger, peeled and roughly
  chopped
450 g/1 lb lean pork mince

4 tbsp freshly chopped
  coriander
1 tsp Chinese five spice
  powder
salt and freshly ground black
  pepper
20 wonton wrappers
1 medium egg, lightly beaten
vegetable oil for deep-frying
chilli sauce, to serve

1 Place the onion, garlic, chilli and ginger in a food processor and blend until very finely chopped. Add the pork, coriander and Chinese five spice powder. Season to taste with salt and pepper, then blend again briefly to mix. Divide the mixture into 20 equal portions and with floured hands shape each into a walnut-sized ball.

2 Brush the edges of a wonton wrapper with beaten egg, place a pork ball in the centre, then bring the corners to the centre and pinch together to make a money bag. Repeat with the remaining pork balls and wrappers.

3 Pour sufficient oil into a heavy-based saucepan or deep-fat fryer so that it is one-third full and heat to 180°C/350°F. Deep-fry the wontons in 3 or 4 batches for 3–4 minutes, or until cooked through and golden

and crisp. Drain on absorbent kitchen paper. Serve the crispy pork wontons immediately, allowing 5 per person, with some chilli sauce for dipping.

HELPFUL HINT

When frying the wontons, use a deep, heavy-based saucepan or special deep-fat fryer fitted with a wire basket. Never fill the pan more than one-third full with oil, then heat over a moderate heat until it reaches the required temperature. Either use a cooking thermometer, or drop a cube of day-old bread into the hot oil. It will turn golden-brown in 45 seconds when the oil is hot enough.

MIXED SATAY STICKS

INGREDIENTS   Serves 4

12 large raw prawns
350 g/12 oz beef rump steak
1 tbsp lemon juice
1 garlic clove, peeled and
  crushed
salt
2 tsp soft dark brown sugar
1 tsp ground cumin
1 tsp ground coriander
¼ tsp ground turmeric
1 tbsp groundnut oil
fresh coriander leaves, to
  garnish

FOR THE SPICY PEANUT SAUCE:
1 shallot, peeled and very
  finely chopped
1 tsp demerara sugar
50 g/2 oz creamed coconut,
  chopped
pinch of chilli powder
1 tbsp dark soy sauce
125 g/4 oz crunchy peanut
  butter

1 Preheat the grill on high just before required. Soak 8 bamboo skewers in cold water for at least 30 minutes. Peel the prawns, leaving the tails on. Using a sharp knife, remove the black vein along the back of the prawns. Cut the beef into 1 cm/½ inch wide strips. Place the prawns and beef in separate bowls and sprinkle each with ½ tablespoon of the lemon juice.

2 Mix together the garlic, pinch of salt, sugar, cumin, coriander, turmeric and groundnut oil to make a paste. Lightly brush over the prawns and beef. Cover and place in the refrigerator to marinate for at least 30 minutes, but for longer if possible.

3 Meanwhile, make the sauce. Pour 125 ml/4 fl oz of water into a small saucepan, add the shallot and sugar and heat gently until the sugar has dissolved. Stir in the creamed coconut and chilli powder. When melted, remove from the heat and stir in the peanut butter. Leave to cool slightly, then spoon into a serving dish.

4 Thread 3 prawns on to each of 4 skewers and divide the sliced beef between the remaining skewers.

5 Cook the skewers under the preheated grill for 4–5 minutes, turning occasionally. The prawns should be opaque and pink and the beef browned on the outside, but still pink in the centre. Transfer to warmed individual serving plates, garnish with a few fresh coriander leaves and serve immediately with the warm peanut sauce.

SWEETCORN FRITTERS

INGREDIENTS   Serves 4

4 tbsp groundnut oil
1 small onion, peeled and
  finely chopped
1 red chilli, deseeded and
  finely chopped
1 garlic clove, peeled and
  crushed
1 tsp ground coriander
325 g can sweetcorn

6 spring onions, trimmed and
  finely sliced
1 medium egg, lightly beaten
salt and freshly ground black
  pepper
3 tbsp plain flour
1 tsp baking powder
spring onion curls, to garnish
Thai-style chutney, to serve

1 Heat 1 tablespoon of the groundnut oil in a frying pan, add the onion and cook gently for 7–8 minutes or until beginning to soften. Add the chilli, garlic and ground coriander and cook for 1 minute, stirring continuously. Remove from the heat.

2 Drain the sweetcorn and tip into a mixing bowl. Lightly mash with a potato masher to break down the corn a little. Add the cooked onion mixture to the bowl with the spring onions and beaten egg. Season to taste with salt and pepper, then stir to mix together. Sift the flour and baking powder over the mixture and stir in.

3 Heat 2 tablespoons of the groundnut oil in a large frying pan. Drop 4 or 5 heaped teaspoonfuls of the sweetcorn mixture into the pan, and using a fish slice or spatula, flatten each to make a 1 cm/½ inch thick fritter.

4 Fry the fritters for 3 minutes, or until golden brown on the underside, turn over and fry for a further 3 minutes, or until cooked through and crisp.

5 Remove the fritters from the pan and drain on absorbent kitchen paper. Keep warm while cooking the remaining fritters, adding a little more oil if needed. Garnish with spring onion curls and serve immediately with a Thai-style chutney.

HELPFUL HINT

To make a spring onion curl, trim off the root and some green top to leave 10 cm/4 inches. Make a 3 cm/1¼ inch cut down from the top, then make another cut at a right angle to the first cut. Continue making fine cuts. Soak the spring onions in iced water for 20 minutes and they open up and curl.

THAI CRAB CAKES

INGREDIENTS
Serves 4

225 g/8 oz white and brown crabmeat (about equivalent to the flesh of 2 medium crabs)
1 tsp ground coriander
¼ tsp chilli powder
¼ tsp ground turmeric
2 tsp lime juice
1 tsp soft light brown sugar
2.5 cm/1 inch piece fresh root ginger, peeled and grated

3 tbsp freshly chopped coriander
2 tsp finely chopped lemon grass
2 tbsp plain flour
2 medium eggs, separated
50 g/2 oz fresh white breadcrumbs
3 tbsp groundnut oil
lime wedges, to garnish
mixed salad leaves, to serve

1 Place the crabmeat in a bowl with the ground coriander, chilli, turmeric, lime juice, sugar, ginger, chopped coriander, lemon grass, flour and egg yolks. Mix together well.

2 Divide the mixture into 12 equal portions and form each into a small patty about 5 cm/ 2 inches across. Lightly whisk the egg whites and put into a dish. Place the breadcrumbs on a separate plate.

3 Dip each crab cake, first in the egg whites, then in the breadcrumbs, turning to coat both sides. Place on a plate, cover and chill in the refrigerator until ready to cook.

4 Heat the oil in a large frying pan. Add 6 crab cakes and cook for 3 minutes on each side, or until crisp and golden brown on the outside and cooked through.

Remove, drain on absorbent kitchen paper and keep warm while cooking the remaining cakes. Arrange on plates, garnish with lime wedges and serve immediately with salad leaves.

HELPFUL HINT

If you buy fresh crabs, prepare them in the following way. Twist off the legs and claws, then crack them open and remove the meat. Turn the crab on to its back and twist off the bony, pointed flap. Place the tip of a knife between the main shell and where the legs were attached, twist the blade to lift up and remove, then scrape out the brown meat. Pull away and discard the soft, grey gills. Split the body in half and using a skewer, remove the white meat from the cavities.

SESAME PRAWN TOASTS

INGREDIENTS   Serves 4

125 g/4 oz peeled cooked
  prawns
1 tbsp cornflour
2 spring onions, peeled and
  roughly chopped
2 tsp freshly grated root ginger
2 tsp dark soy sauce
pinch of Chinese five-spice
  powder (optional)

1 small egg, beaten
salt and freshly ground black
  pepper
6 thin slices day-old white
  bread
40 g/1½ oz sesame seeds
vegetable oil for deep-frying
chilli sauce, to serve

1 Place the prawns in a food processor or blender with the cornflour, spring onions, ginger, soy sauce and Chinese five spice powder, if using. Blend to a fairly smooth paste. Spoon into a bowl and stir in the beaten egg. Season to taste with salt and pepper.

2 Cut the crusts off the bread. Spread the prawn paste in an even layer on one side of each slice. Sprinkle over the sesame seeds and press down lightly.

3 Cut each slice diagonally into 4 triangles. Place on a board and chill in the refrigerator for 30 minutes.

4 Pour sufficient oil into a heavy-based saucepan or deep-fat fryer so that it is one-third full. Heat until it reaches a temperature of 180°C/350°F. Cook the toasts in batches of 5 or 6, carefully lowering them seeded-side down into the oil. Deep-fry for 2–3 minutes, or until lightly browned, then turn over and cook for 1 minute more. Using a slotted spoon, lift out the toasts and drain on absorbent kitchen paper. Keep warm while frying the remaining toasts. Arrange on a warmed platter and serve immediately with some chilli sauce for dipping.

HELPFUL HINT

The toasts can be prepared to the end of step 3 up to 12 hours in advance. Cover and chill in the refrigerator until needed. It is important to use bread that is a day or two old and not fresh bread. Make sure that the prawns are well-drained before puréeing – pat them dry on absorbent kitchen paper, if necessary.

SWEET-&-SOUR BATTERED FISH

INGREDIENTS   Serves 4–6

450 g/1 lb cod fillet, skinned
150 g/5 oz plain flour
salt and freshly ground black
  pepper
2 tbsp cornflour
2 tbsp arrowroot
vegetable oil for deep-frying

**FOR THE SWEET-&-SOUR
  SAUCE:**
4 tbsp orange juice
2 tbsp white wine vinegar

2 tbsp dry sherry
1 tbsp dark soy sauce
1 tbsp soft light brown sugar
2 tsp tomato purée
1 red pepper, deseeded and
  diced
2 tsp cornflour

1 Cut the fish into pieces about 5 cm x 2.5 cm/2 x 1 inch. Place 4 tablespoons of the flour in a small bowl, season with salt and pepper to taste, then add the fish strips a few at a time and toss until coated.

2 Sift the remaining flour into a bowl with a pinch of salt, the cornflour and arrowroot. Gradually whisk in 300 ml/½ pint iced water to make a smooth, thin batter.

3 Heat the oil in a wok or deep-fat fryer to 190°C/ 375°F. Working in batches, dip the fish strips in the batter and deep-fry them for 3–5 minutes, or until crisp. Using a slotted spoon, remove the strips and drain on absorbent kitchen paper.

4 Meanwhile, make the sauce. Place 3 tablespoons of the

orange juice, the vinegar, sherry, soy sauce, sugar, tomato purée and red pepper in a small saucepan. Bring to the boil, lower the heat and simmer for 3 minutes.

5 Blend the cornflour with the remaining orange juice, stir into the sauce and simmer, stirring, for 1 minute or until thickened. Arrange the fish on a warmed platter or individual plates. Drizzle a little of the sauce over and serve immediately with the remaining sauce.

TASTY TIP

Any firm white fish can be used for this dish, as long as it is fairly thick. Your fish-monger can tell you which varieties are suitable.

SPICY BEEF PANCAKES

INGREDIENTS
Serves 4

50 g/2 oz plain flour
pinch of salt
½ tsp Chinese five spice
 powder
1 large egg yolk
150 ml/¼ pint milk
4 tsp sunflower oil
slices of spring onion, to
 garnish

FOR THE SPICY BEEF FILLING:
1 tbsp sesame oil
4 spring onions, sliced

1 cm/½ inch piece fresh root
 ginger, peeled and grated
1 garlic clove, peeled and
 crushed
300 g/11 oz sirloin steak,
 trimmed and cut into strips
1 red chilli, deseeded and
 finely chopped
1 tsp sherry vinegar
1 tsp soft dark brown sugar
1 tbsp dark soy sauce

1 Sift the flour, salt and Chinese five spice powder into a bowl and make a well in the centre. Add the egg yolk and a little of the milk. Gradually beat in, drawing in the flour to make a smooth batter. Whisk in the rest of the milk.

2 Heat 1 teaspoon of the sunflower oil in a small heavy-based frying pan. Pour in just enough batter to thinly coat the base of the pan. Cook over a medium heat for 1 minute, or until the underside of the pancake is golden brown.

3 Turn or toss the pancake and cook for 1 minute, or until the other side of the pancake is golden brown. Make 7 more pancakes with the remaining batter. Stack them on a warmed plate as you make them, with greaseproof paper between each pancake. Cover with tinfoil and keep warm in a low oven.

4 Make the filling. Heat a wok or large frying pan, add the sesame oil and when hot, add the spring onions, ginger and garlic and stir-fry for 1 minute. Add the beef strips, stir-fry for 3–4 minutes, then stir in the chilli, vinegar, sugar and soy sauce. Cook for 1 minute, then remove from the heat.

5 Spoon one-eighth of the filling over one half of each pancake. Fold the pancakes in half, then fold in half again. Garnish with a few slices of spring onion and serve immediately.

LION'S HEAD PORK BALLS

INGREDIENTS   Serves 4

75 g/3 oz glutinous rice
450 g/1 lb lean pork mince
2 garlic cloves, peeled and
   crushed
1 tbsp cornflour
½ tsp Chinese five spice powder
2 tsp dark soy sauce
1 tbsp Chinese rice wine or
   dry sherry
2 tbsp freshly chopped
   coriander
salt and freshly ground black
   pepper

**FOR THE SWEET CHILLI
DIPPING SAUCE:**

2 tsp caster sugar
1 tbsp sherry vinegar
1 tbsp light soy sauce
1 shallot, peeled and very
   finely chopped
1 small red chilli, deseeded
   and finely chopped
2 tsp sesame oil

1 Place the rice in a bowl and pour over plenty of cold water. Cover and soak for 2 hours. Tip into a sieve and drain well.

2 Place the pork, garlic, cornflour, Chinese five spice powder, soy sauce, Chinese rice wine or sherry and coriander in a bowl. Season to taste with salt and pepper and mix together.

3 With slightly wet hands, shape the pork mixture into 20 walnut-sized balls, then roll in the rice to coat. Place the balls slightly apart in a steamer or a colander set over a saucepan of boiling water, cover and steam for 20 minutes, or until cooked through.

4 Meanwhile, make the dipping sauce. Stir together the sugar, vinegar and soy sauce until the sugar dissolves. Add the shallot, chilli and sesame oil and whisk together with a fork. Transfer to a small serving bowl, cover and leave to stand for at least 10 minutes before serving.

5 Remove the pork balls from the steamer and arrange them on a warmed serving platter. Serve immediately with the sweet chilli dipping sauce.

FOOD FACT

These meatballs get their name from the rice coating, which is thought to resemble a lion's mane. Glutinous rice, sometimes labelled sticky rice, has a high starch content. Its name is descriptive of its nature, as the grains stick together when cooked.

HOT-&-SOUR SQUID

INGREDIENTS

Serves 4

8 baby squid, cleaned
2 tbsp dark soy sauce
2 tbsp hoisin sauce
1 tbsp lime juice
2 tbsp dry sherry
1 tbsp clear honey
2.5 cm/1 inch piece fresh root ginger, peeled and finely chopped

1 red chilli, deseeded and finely chopped
1 green chilli, deseeded and finely chopped
1 tsp cornflour
salt and freshly ground black pepper
vegetable oil for deep-frying
lime wedges, to garnish

1 Slice open the body of each squid lengthways, open out and place on a chopping board with the inside uppermost. Using a sharp knife, score lightly in a criss-cross pattern. Cut each one into 4 pieces. Trim the tentacles.

2 Place the soy and hoisin sauces with the lime juice, sherry, honey, ginger, chillies and cornflour in a bowl. Season to taste with salt and pepper and mix together. Add the squid, stir well to coat, then cover and place in the refrigerator to marinate for 1 hour.

3 Tip the squid into a sieve over a small saucepan and strain off the marinade. Scrape any bits of chilli or ginger into the saucepan, as they would burn if fried.

4 Fill a deep-fat fryer one-third full with oil and heat to 180°C/350°F. Deep-fry the squid in batches for 2–3 minutes or until golden and crisp. Remove the squid and drain on absorbent kitchen paper. Keep warm.

5 Bring the marinade to the boil and let it bubble gently for a few seconds. Arrange the squid on a warmed serving dish and drizzle over the marinade. Garnish with lime wedges and serve immediately.

HELPFUL HINT

It is simple to prepare squid. Rinse well in cold water, then firmly pull apart the head and body; the innards will come away with the head. Remove and discard the transparent beak. Rinse the body pouch thoroughly under cold running water and peel off the thin layer of dark skin. The tentacles are edible, so cut them away from the head just below the eyes. They can also be deep-fried to be used in this dish, if liked.

AROMATIC QUAIL EGGS

INGREDIENTS   Serves 6

2 tbsp jasmine tea leaves
24 quail eggs
2 tsp salt
4 tbsp dark soy sauce
1 tbsp soft dark brown sugar
2 whole star anise
1 cinnamon stick

2 tbsp sherry vinegar
2 tbsp Chinese rice wine or
  dry sherry
2 tbsp caster sugar
¼ tsp Chinese five spice
  powder
¼ tsp cornflour

1 Place the tea leaves in a jug and pour over 150 ml/¼ pint boiling water. Leave to stand for 5 minutes, then strain, reserving the tea and discarding the leaves.

2 Meanwhile, place the eggs in a saucepan with just enough cold water to cover them. Bring to the boil and simmer for 1 minute. Using a slotted spoon, move the eggs and roll them gently to just crack the shells all over.

3 Add the salt, 2 tablespoons of the soy sauce, the dark brown sugar, star anise and cinnamon stick to the egg cooking water and pour in the tea. Bring to the boil, return the eggs to the saucepan and simmer for 1 minute. Remove from the heat and leave the eggs for 2 minutes, then remove the eggs and plunge them into cold water. Leave the tea mixture to cool.

4 Return the eggs to the cooled tea mixture, leave for 30 minutes, then drain and remove the shells to reveal the marbling.

5 Pour the remaining soy sauce, the vinegar and Chinese rice wine or sherry into a small saucepan and add the caster sugar and Chinese five-spice powder. Blend the cornflour with 1 tablespoon of cold water and stir into the soy sauce mixture. Heat until boiling and slightly thickened, stirring continuously. Leave to cool.

6 Pour the sauce into a small serving dish. Place the eggs in a serving bowl or divide between individual plates and serve with the dipping sauce.

TASTY TIP

This recipe can also be used to marble and flavour ordinary eggs. Allowing 9 eggs to serve 6 people, simmer for 4 minutes in step 2 and for a further 4 minutes in step 3. Leave the eggs to soak and peel as before, then cut widthways into quarters when serving.

SPICY PRAWNS IN LETTUCE CUPS

INGREDIENTS   Serves 4

1 lemon grass stalk
225 g/8 oz peeled cooked
    prawns
1 tsp finely grated lime zest
1 red bird's-eye chilli,
    deseeded and finely
    chopped
2.5 cm/1 inch piece fresh root
    ginger, peeled and grated
2 Little Gem lettuces, divided
    into leaves
25 g/1 oz roasted peanuts,
    chopped

2 spring onions, trimmed and
    diagonally sliced
sprig of fresh coriander, to
    garnish

FOR THE COCONUT SAUCE:
2 tbsp freshly grated or
    unsweetened shredded
    coconut
1 tbsp hoisin sauce
1 tbsp light soy sauce
1 tbsp Thai fish sauce
1 tbsp palm sugar or soft light
    brown sugar

1 Remove 3 or 4 of the tougher outer leaves of the lemon grass and reserve for another dish. Finely chop the remaining softer centre. Place 2 teaspoons of the chopped lemon grass in a bowl with the prawns, grated lime zest, chilli and ginger. Mix together to coat the prawns. Cover and place in the refrigerator to marinate while you make the coconut sauce.

2 For the sauce, place the grated coconut in a wok or nonstick frying pan and dry-fry for 2–3 minutes or until golden. Remove from the pan and reserve. Add the hoisin, soy and fish sauces to the pan with the sugar and 4 tablespoons of water. Simmer for 2–3 minutes, then remove from the heat. Leave to cool.

3 Pour the sauce over the prawns, add the toasted coconut and toss to mix together. Divide the prawn and coconut sauce mixture between the lettuce leaves and arrange on a platter.

4 Sprinkle over the chopped roasted peanuts and spring onions and garnish with a sprig of fresh coriander. Serve immediately.

HELPFUL HINT

Instead of lettuce leaves you can use radicchio, chicory or flatter *miang* leaves, available from Thai grocery stores.

CANTONESE CHICKEN WINGS

INGREDIENTS

Serves 4

3 tbsp hoisin sauce

2 tbsp dark soy sauce

1 tbsp sesame oil

1 garlic clove, peeled and crushed

2.5 cm/1 inch piece fresh root ginger, peeled and grated

1 tbsp Chinese rice wine or dry sherry

2 tsp chilli bean sauce

2 tsp red or white wine vinegar

2 tbsp soft light brown sugar

900 g/2 lb large chicken wings

50 g/2 oz cashew nuts, chopped

2 spring onions, trimmed and finely chopped

1 Preheat the oven to 220°C/425°F/Gas Mark 7, 15 minutes before cooking. Place the hoisin sauce, soy sauce, sesame oil, garlic, ginger, Chinese rice wine or sherry, chilli bean sauce, vinegar and sugar in a small saucepan with 6 tablespoons of water. Bring to the boil, stirring occasionally, then simmer for about 30 seconds. Remove the glaze from the heat.

2 Place the chicken wings in a roasting tin in a single layer. Pour over the glaze and stir until the wings are coated thoroughly.

3 Cover the tin loosely with tinfoil, place in the preheated oven and roast for 25 minutes. Remove the tinfoil, baste the wings and cook for a further 5 minutes.

4 Reduce the oven temperature to 190°C/375°F/Gas Mark 5. Turn the wings over and sprinkle with the chopped cashew nuts and spring onions. Return to the oven and cook for 5 minutes, or until the nuts are lightly browned, the glaze is sticky and the wings are tender. Remove from the oven and leave to stand for 5 minutes before arranging on a warmed platter. Serve immediately with finger bowls and plenty of napkins.

HELPFUL HINT

Chicken wings are regarded as a delicacy in both China and Thailand and are considered one of the tastiest parts of the bird. If you give your butcher advance notice, he will probably sell them to you very cheaply, as they are often trimmed off and discarded when cutting chickens into portions.

VEGETABLE THAI SPRING ROLLS

INGREDIENTS   Serves 4

50 g/2 oz cellophane vermicelli
4 dried shiitake mushrooms
1 tbsp groundnut oil
2 medium carrots, peeled and
  cut into fine matchsticks
125 g/4 oz mangetout, cut
  lengthways into fine strips
3 spring onions, trimmed and
  chopped
125 g/4 oz canned bamboo
  shoots, cut into fine
  matchsticks

1 cm/½ inch piece fresh root
  ginger, peeled and grated
1 tbsp light soy sauce
1 medium egg, separated
salt and freshly ground black
  pepper
20 spring roll wrappers, each
  about 12.5 cm/5 inch square
vegetable oil for deep-frying
spring onion tassels, to
  garnish

1 Place the vermicelli in a bowl and pour over enough boiling water to cover. Leave to soak for 5 minutes or until softened, then drain. Cut into 7.5 cm/3 inch lengths. Soak the shiitake mushrooms in almost boiling water for 15 minutes, drain, discard the stalks and slice thinly.

2 Heat a wok or large frying pan, add the groundnut oil and when hot, add the carrots and stir-fry for 1 minute. Add the mangetout and spring onions and stir-fry for 2–3 minutes or until tender. Tip the vegetables into a bowl and leave to cool.

3 Stir the vermicelli and shiitake mushrooms into the cooled vegetables with the bamboo shoots, ginger, soy sauce and egg yolk. Season to taste with salt and pepper and mix thoroughly.

4 Brush the edges of a spring roll wrapper with a little beaten egg white. Spoon 2 teaspoons of the vegetable filling on to the wrapper, in a 7.5 cm/3 inch log shape 2.5 cm/1 inch from one edge. Fold the wrapper edge over the filling, then fold in the right and left sides. Brush the folded edges with more egg white and roll up neatly. Place on an oiled baking sheet, seam-side down and make the rest of the spring rolls.

5 Heat the oil in a heavy-based saucepan or deep-fat fryer to 180°C/350°F. Deep-fry the spring rolls, 6 at a time for 2–3 minutes, or until golden brown and crisp. Drain on absorbent kitchen paper and arrange on a warmed platter. Garnish with spring onion tassels and serve immediately.

CRISPY PRAWNS WITH CHINESE DIPPING SAUCE

INGREDIENTS   Serves 4

450 g/1 lb medium-sized raw
  prawns, peeled
¼ tsp salt
6 tbsp groundnut oil
2 garlic cloves, peeled and
  finely chopped
2.5 cm/1 inch piece fresh root
  ginger, peeled and finely
  chopped
1 green chilli, deseeded and
  finely chopped

4 stems fresh coriander, leaves
  and stems roughly chopped

**FOR THE CHINESE DIPPING
  SAUCE:**
3 tbsp dark soy sauce
3 tbsp rice wine vinegar
1 tbsp caster sugar
2 tbsp chilli oil
2 spring onions, finely
  shredded

1 Using a sharp knife, remove the black vein along the back of the prawns. Sprinkle the prawns with the salt and leave to stand for 15 minutes. Pat dry on absorbent kitchen paper.

2 Heat a wok or large frying pan, add the groundnut oil and when hot, add the prawns and stir-fry in 2 batches for about 1 minute, or until they turn pink and are almost cooked. Using a slotted spoon, remove the prawns and keep warm in a low oven.

3 Drain the oil from the wok, leaving 1 tablespoon. Add the garlic, ginger and chilli and cook for about 30 seconds. Add the coriander, return the prawns and stir-fry for 1–2 minutes, or until the prawns are cooked through and the garlic is golden. Turn into a warmed serving dish.

4 For the dipping sauce, using a fork, beat together the soy sauce, rice vinegar, caster sugar and chilli oil in a small bowl. Stir in the spring onions. Serve immediately with the hot prawns.

TASTY TIP

Although you must cook raw prawns thoroughly, it is equally important not to overcook them or they will become tough and chewy and lose their delicate flavour. Stir-fry them until they are pink and opaque, constantly moving them around the pan, so that they cook evenly. They will only need cooking briefly in step 3.

POACHED FISH DUMPLINGS WITH CREAMY CHILLI SAUCE

INGREDIENTS   Serves 4

450 g/1 lb white fish fillet,
    skinned and boned
1 tsp dark soy sauce
1 tbsp cornflour
1 medium egg yolk
salt and freshly ground black
    pepper
3 tbsp freshly chopped
    coriander, plus extra, to
    garnish
1.6 litres/2¾ pints fish stock

**FOR THE CREAMY CHILLI
    SAUCE:**
2 tsp groundnut oil
2 garlic cloves, peeled and
    finely chopped
4 spring onions, trimmed and
    finely sliced
2 tbsp dry sherry
1 tbsp sweet chilli sauce
1 tbsp light soy sauce
1 tbsp lemon juice
6 tbsp crème fraîche

TO GARNISH:
sprigs of fresh coriander
fresh carrot sticks

1 Chop the fish into chunks and place in a food processor with the soy sauce, cornflour and egg yolk. Season to taste with salt and pepper. Blend until fairly smooth. Add the coriander and process for a few seconds until well mixed. Transfer to a bowl, cover and chill in the refrigerator for 30 minutes.

2 With damp hands shape the chilled mixture into walnut-sized balls and place on a baking tray lined with nonstick baking paper. Chill in the refrigerator for a further 30 minutes.

3 Pour the stock into a wide saucepan, bring to the boil, then reduce the heat until barely simmering. Add the fish balls and poach for 3–4 minutes or until cooked through.

4 Meanwhile, make the sauce. Heat the oil in a small saucepan, add the garlic and spring onions and cook until golden. Stir in the sherry, chilli and soy sauces and lemon juice, then remove immediately from the heat. Stir in the crème fraîche and season to taste with salt and pepper.

5 Using a slotted spoon, lift the cooked fish balls from the stock and place on a warmed serving dish. Drizzle over the sauce, garnish with sprigs of fresh coriander and serve immediately.

STEAMED MONKFISH WITH CHILLI & GINGER

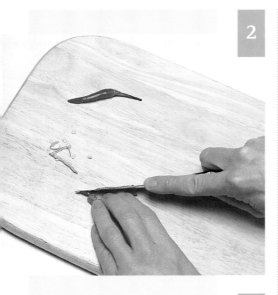

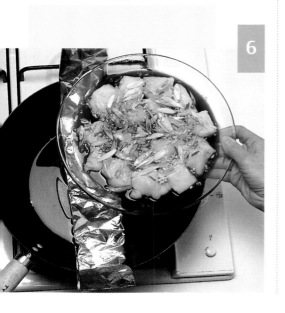

INGREDIENTS   Serves 4

700 g/1½ lb skinless monkfish
  tail
1–2 red chillies
4 cm/1½ inch piece fresh root
  ginger
1 tsp sesame oil
4 spring onions, trimmed and
  thinly sliced diagonally

2 tbsp soy sauce
2 tbsp Chinese rice wine or
  dry sherry
freshly steamed rice, to serve

TO GARNISH:
sprigs of fresh coriander
lime wedges

1 Place the monkfish on a chopping board. Using a sharp knife, cut down each side of the central bone and remove. Cut the fish into 2.5cm/1 inch pieces and reserve.

2 Make a slit down the side of each chilli, remove and discard the seeds and the membrane, then slice thinly. Peel the ginger and either chop finely or grate.

3 Brush a large heatproof plate with the sesame oil and arrange the monkfish pieces in one layer on the plate. Sprinkle over the spring onions and pour over the soy sauce and Chinese rice wine or sherry.

4 Place a wire rack or inverted ramekin in a large wok. Pour in enough water to come about 2.5 cm/1 inch up the side of the wok and bring to the boil over a high heat.

5 Fold a long piece of tinfoil lengthways to about 5–7.5 cm/2–3 inches wide and lay it over the rack or ramekin. It must extend beyond the plate edge when it is placed in the wok.

6 Place the plate with the monkfish on the rack or ramekin and cover tightly. Steam over a medium-low heat for 5 minutes, or until the fish is tender and opaque. Using the tinfoil as a hammock, lift out the plate. Garnish with sprigs of coriander and lime wedges and serve immediately with steamed rice.

FOOD FACT

Chillies immediately transformed Chinese cooking when they were introduced to China about 100 years ago. They are used extensively in Szechuan and in Hunan.

RED PRAWN CURRY WITH JASMINE-SCENTED RICE

INGREDIENTS   Serves 4

½ tbsp coriander seeds

1 tsp cumin seeds

1 tsp black peppercorns

½ tsp salt

1–2 dried red chillies

2 shallots, peeled and chopped

3–4 garlic cloves

2.5 cm/1 inch piece fresh galangal or root ginger, peeled and chopped

1 kaffir lime leaf or 1 tsp kaffir lime rind

½ tsp red chilli powder

½ tbsp shrimp paste

1–1½ lemon grass stalks, outer leaves removed and thinly sliced

750 ml/1¼ pints coconut milk

1 red chilli deseeded and thinly sliced

2 tbsp Thai fish sauce

2 tsp soft brown sugar

1 red pepper, deseeded and thinly sliced

550 g/1¼ lb large peeled tiger prawns

2 fresh lime leaves, shredded (optional)

2 tbsp fresh mint leaves, shredded

2 tbsp Thai or Italian basil leaves, shredded

freshly cooked Thai fragrant rice, to serve

1 Using a pestle and mortar or a spice grinder, grind the coriander and cumin seeds, peppercorns and salt to a fine powder. Add the dried chillies one at a time and grind to a fine powder.

2 Place the shallots, garlic, galangal or ginger, kaffir lime leaf or rind, chilli powder and shrimp paste in a food processor. Add the ground spices and process until a thick paste forms. Scrape down the bowl once or twice, adding a few drops of water if the mixture is too thick and not forming a paste. Stir in the lemon grass.

3 Transfer the paste to a large wok and cook over a medium heat for 2–3 minutes or until fragrant.

4 Stir in the coconut milk, bring to the boil, then lower the heat and simmer for about 10 minutes. Add the chilli, fish sauce, sugar and red pepper and simmer for 15 minutes.

5 Stir in the prawns and cook for 5 minutes, or until the prawns are pink and tender. Stir in the shredded herbs, heat for a further minute and serve immediately with the cooked rice.

THAI PRAWN & RICE NOODLE SALAD

INGREDIENTS · Serves 4

75 g/3 oz rice vermicelli

175 g/6 oz mangetout, cut in half crossways

½ cucumber, peeled, deseeded and diced

2–3 spring onions, trimmed and thinly sliced diagonally

16–20 large cooked tiger prawns, peeled with tails left on

2 tbsp chopped unsalted peanuts or cashews

3 tbsp Thai fish sauce

1 tbsp sugar

2.5 cm/1 inch piece fresh root ginger, peeled and finely chopped

1 red chilli, deseeded and thinly sliced

3–4 tbsp freshly chopped coriander or mint

TO GARNISH:

lime wedges

sprigs of fresh mint

FOR THE DRESSING:

4 tbsp freshly squeezed lime juice

1 Place the vermicelli in a bowl and pour over hot water to cover. Leave to stand for 5 minutes or until softened. Drain, rinse, then drain again and reserve.

2 Meanwhile, mix all the dressing ingredients in a large bowl until well blended and the sugar has dissolved. Reserve.

3 Bring a medium saucepan of water to the boil. Add the mangetout, return to the boil and cook for 30–50 seconds. Drain, refresh under cold running water, drain again and reserve.

4 Stir the cucumber, spring onions and all but 4 of the prawns into the dressing until coated lightly. Add the mangetout and noodles and toss until all the ingredients are mixed evenly.

5 Spoon the noodle salad on to warmed individual plates. Sprinkle with peanuts or cashews and garnish each dish with a reserved prawn, a lime wedge and a sprig of mint.

FOOD FACT

Thai fish sauce, or *nam pla*, adds a richness to many dishes. The fishy flavour virtually disappears when cooked.

THAI CURRIED SEAFOOD

INGREDIENTS   Serves 6-8

2 tbsp vegetable oil
450 g/1 lb scallops, with coral
    attached if preferred, halved
    if large
1 onion, peeled and finely
    chopped
4 garlic cloves, peeled and
    finely chopped
5 cm/2 inch piece fresh root
    ginger, peeled and finely
    chopped
1–2 red chillies, deseeded and
    thinly sliced
1–2 tbsp curry paste (hot or
    medium, to taste)
1 tsp ground coriander
1 tsp ground cumin
1 lemon grass stalk, bruised

225 g can chopped tomatoes
125 ml/4 fl oz chicken stock or
    water
450 ml/¾ pint coconut milk
12 live mussels, scrubbed and
    beards removed
450 g/1 lb cooked peeled
    prawns
225 g/8 oz frozen or canned
    crabmeat, drained
2 tbsp freshly chopped
    coriander
freshly shredded coconut, to
    garnish (optional)
freshly cooked rice or rice
    noodles, to serve

1 Heat a wok or large frying pan, add 1 tablespoon of the oil and when hot, add the scallops and stir-fry for 2 minutes or until opaque and firm. Transfer to a plate with any juices.

2 Heat the remaining oil. Add the onion, garlic, ginger and chillies and stir-fry for 1 minute or until they begin to soften.

3 Add the curry paste, coriander, cumin and lemon grass and stir-fry for 2 minutes. Add the tomatoes and stock, bring to the boil then simmer for 5 minutes or until reduced, stirring constantly. Stir in the coconut milk and simmer for 2 minutes.

4 Stir in the mussels, cover and simmer for 2 minutes or until they begin to open. Stir in the prawns, crabmeat and reserved scallops with any juices and cook for 2 minutes or until heated through. Discard the lemon grass and any unopened mussels. Stir in the chopped coriander. Tip into a large warmed serving dish and garnish with the coconut, if using. Serve immediately with rice or noodles.

HELPFUL HINT

When preparing live mussels, discard any that don't close when tapped sharply.

FRIED FISH WITH THAI CHILLI DIPPING SAUCE

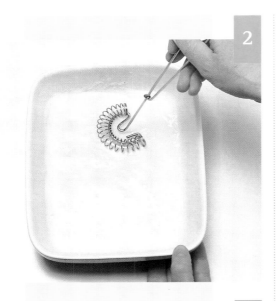

INGREDIENTS   Serves 4

1 large egg white
½ tsp curry powder or turmeric
3–4 tbsp cornflour
salt and freshly ground black
    pepper
4 plaice or sole fillets, about
    225 g/8 oz each
300 ml/½ pint vegetable oil

FOR THE DIPPING SAUCE:
2 red chillies, deseeded and
    thinly sliced

2 shallots, peeled and finely
    chopped
1 tbsp freshly squeezed lime
    juice
3 tbsp Thai fish sauce
1 tbsp freshly chopped
    coriander or Thai basil

TO SERVE:
freshly cooked rice
mixed salad leaves

1 To make the dipping sauce, combine all the ingredients in a bowl. Leave for at least 15 minutes.

2 Beat the egg white until frothy and whisk into a shallow dish.

3 Stir the curry powder or turmeric into the cornflour in a bowl and season to taste with salt and pepper. Dip each fish fillet in the beaten egg white, dust lightly on both sides with the cornflour mixture and place on a wire rack.

4 Heat a wok or large frying pan, add the oil and heat to 180°C/350°F. Add 1 or 2 fillets and fry for 5 minutes, or until crisp and golden, turning once during cooking.

5 Using a slotted spatula, carefully remove the cooked fish and drain on absorbent kitchen paper. Keep warm while frying the remaining fillets.

6 Arrange the fillets on warmed individual plates and serve immediately with the dipping sauce, rice and salad.

HELPFUL HINT

To prepare fresh chillies, slit them lengthways with a small sharp knife, then remove and discard the seeds, unless you want a really fiery dish. Wash your hands thoroughly with soap and water as the volatile oils can cause irritation.

SCALLOPS & PRAWNS BRAISED IN LEMON GRASS

INGREDIENTS

Serves 4–6

450 g/1 lb large raw prawns, peeled with tails left on
350 g/12 oz scallops, with coral attached
2 red chillies, deseeded and coarsely chopped
2 garlic cloves, peeled and coarsely chopped
4 shallots, peeled
1 tbsp shrimp paste

2 tbsp freshly chopped coriander
400 ml/14 fl oz coconut milk
2–3 lemon grass stalks, outer leaves discarded and bruised
2 tbsp Thai fish sauce
1 tbsp sugar
freshly steamed basmati rice, to serve

1 Rinse the prawns and scallops and pat dry with absorbent kitchen paper. Using a sharp knife, remove the black vein along the back of the prawns. Reserve.

2 Place the chillies, garlic, shallots, shrimp paste and 1 tablespoon of the chopped coriander in a food processor. Add 1 tablespoon of the coconut milk and 2 tablespoons of water and blend to form a thick paste. Reserve the chilli paste.

3 Pour the remaining coconut milk with 3 tablespoons of water into a large wok or frying pan, add the lemon grass and bring to the boil. Simmer over a medium heat for 10 minutes or until reduced slightly.

4 Stir the chilli paste, fish sauce and sugar into the coconut

milk and continue to simmer for 2 minutes, stirring occasionally.

5 Add the prepared prawns and scallops and simmer gently, for 3 minutes, stirring occasionally, or until cooked and the prawns are pink and the scallops are opaque.

6 Remove the lemon grass and stir in the remaining chopped coriander. Serve immediately spooned over freshly steamed basmati rice.

FOOD FACT

Shrimp paste is made from fermented, salted shrimp purée that has been dried in the sun. It should be blended with a little water before use. Shrimp sauce, which is not dried, can be substituted.

FRAGRANT THAI SWORDFISH WITH PEPPERS

INGREDIENTS

Serves 4–6

550 g/1¼ lb swordfish, cut into 5 cm/2 inch strips
2 tbsp vegetable oil
2 lemon grass stalks, peeled, bruised and cut into 2.5 cm/1 inch pieces
2.5 cm/1 inch piece fresh root ginger, peeled and thinly sliced
4–5 shallots, peeled and thinly sliced
2–3 garlic cloves, peeled and thinly sliced
1 small red pepper, deseeded and thinly sliced
1 small yellow pepper, deseeded and thinly sliced

2 tbsp soy sauce
2 tbsp Chinese rice wine or dry sherry
1–2 tsp sugar
1 tsp sesame oil
1 tbsp Thai or Italian basil, shredded
salt and freshly ground black pepper
1 tbsp toasted sesame seeds

FOR THE MARINADE:
1 tbsp soy sauce
1 tbsp Chinese rice wine or dry sherry
1 tbsp sesame oil
1 tbsp cornflour

1 Blend all the marinade ingredients together in a shallow, nonmetallic baking dish. Add the swordfish and spoon the marinade over the fish. Cover and leave to marinate in the refrigerator for at least 30 minutes.

2 Using a slotted spatula or spoon, remove the swordfish from the marinade and drain briefly on absorbent kitchen paper. Heat a wok or large frying pan, add the oil and when hot, add the swordfish and stir-fry for 2 minutes, or until it begins to brown. Remove the swordfish and drain on absorbent kitchen paper.

3 Add the lemon grass, ginger, shallots and garlic to the wok and stir-fry for 30 seconds. Add the peppers, soy sauce, Chinese rice wine or sherry and sugar and stir-fry for 3–4 minutes.

4 Return the swordfish to the wok and stir-fry gently for 1–2 minutes, or until heated through and coated with the sauce. If necessary, moisten the sauce with a little of the marinade or some water. Stir in the sesame oil and the basil and season to taste with salt and pepper. Tip into a warmed serving bowl, sprinkle with sesame seeds and serve immediately.

THAI COCONUT CRAB CURRY

INGREDIENTS   Serves 4–6

1 onion
4 garlic cloves
5 cm/2 inch piece fresh root ginger
2 tbsp vegetable oil
2–3 tsp hot curry paste
400 g/14 oz coconut milk
2 large dressed crabs, white and dark meat separated

2 lemon grass stalks, peeled and bruised
6 spring onions, trimmed and chopped
2 tbsp freshly shredded Thai basil or mint, plus extra, to garnish
freshly boiled rice, to serve

1 Peel the onion and chop finely. Peel the garlic cloves, then either crush or finely chop. Peel the ginger and either grate coarsely or cut into very thin shreds. Reserve.

2 Heat a wok or large frying pan, add the oil and when hot, add the onion, garlic and ginger and stir-fry for 2 minutes, or until the onion is beginning to soften. Stir in the curry paste and stir-fry for 1 minute.

3 Stir the coconut milk into the vegetable mixture with the dark crabmeat. Add the lemon grass, then bring the mixture slowly to the boil, stirring frequently.

4 Add the spring onions and simmer gently for 15 minutes or until the sauce has thickened. Remove and discard the lemon grass stalks.

5 Add the white crabmeat and the shredded basil or mint and stir very gently for 1–2 minutes or until heated through and piping hot. Try to prevent the crabmeat from breaking up.

6 Spoon the curry over boiled rice on warmed individual plates, sprinkle with basil or mint leaves and serve immediately.

FOOD FACT

Lemon grass should be bruised to release its distinctive lemon flavour and scent. This is done by placing it on a chopping board and gently hitting it 2 or 3 times with a rolling pin. For a stronger flavour, the outer leaves can be stripped away and the heart chopped finely. If it is unavailable, a thin strip of lime or lemon rind makes a good alternative.

THAI MARINATED PRAWNS

INGREDIENTS
Serves 4

700 g/1½ lb large raw prawns, peeled with tails left on
2 large eggs
salt
50 g/2 oz cornflour
vegetable oil for deep-frying
lime wedges, to garnish

FOR THE MARINADE:
2 lemon grass stalks, outer leaves discarded and bruised

2 garlic cloves, peeled and finely chopped
2 shallots, peeled and finely chopped
1 red chilli, deseeded and chopped
grated zest and juice of 1 small lime
400 ml/14 fl oz coconut milk

1 Mix all the marinade ingredients together in a bowl, pressing on the solid ingredients to release their flavours. Season to taste with salt and reserve.

2 Using a sharp knife, remove the black vein along the back of the prawns and pat dry with absorbent kitchen paper. Add the prawns to the marinade and stir gently until coated evenly. Leave in the marinade for at least 1 hour, stirring occasionally.

3 Beat the eggs in a deep bowl with a little salt. Place the cornflour in a shallow bowl. Using a slotted spoon or spatula, transfer the prawns from the marinade to the cornflour. Stir gently until the prawns are coated on all sides and shake off any excess.

4 Holding each prawn by its tail, dip it into the beaten egg, then into the cornflour again, shaking off any excess.

5 Pour enough oil into a large wok to come 5 cm/2 inches up the sides and place over a high heat. Working in batches of 5 or 6, deep-fry the prawns for 2 minutes, or until pink and crisp, turning once. Using a slotted spoon, remove and drain on absorbent kitchen paper. Keep warm. Arrange on a warmed serving plate and garnish with lime wedges. Serve immediately.

TASTY TIP

Use vegetable or groundnut oil with a high smoke point here. For extra flavour, add 1–2 tablespoons of garlic, chilli or lemon oil. Make sure the oil is hot enough to cook the prawns quickly, or they will become tough.

WARM LOBSTER SALAD WITH HOT THAI DRESSING

INGREDIENTS
Serves 4

1 orange
50 g/2 oz granulated sugar
2 Cos lettuce hearts, shredded
1 small avocado, peeled and thinly sliced
½ cucumber, peeled, deseeded and thinly sliced
1 ripe mango, peeled, stoned and thinly sliced
1 tbsp butter or vegetable oil
1 large lobster, meat removed and cut into bite-sized pieces
2 tbsp Thai or Italian basil leaves
4 large cooked prawns, peeled with tails left on, to garnish

FOR THE DRESSING:
1 tbsp vegetable oil
4–6 spring onions, trimmed and sliced diagonally into 5 cm/2 inch pieces
2.5 cm/1 inch piece fresh root ginger, peeled and grated
1 garlic clove, peeled and crushed
grated zest of 1 lime
juice of 2–3 small limes
2 tbsp Thai fish sauce
1 tbsp brown sugar
1–2 tsp sweet chilli sauce, or to taste
1 tbsp sesame oil

1 With a sharp knife, cut the orange rind into thin julienne strips, then cook in boiling water for 2 minutes.

2 Drain the orange strips, then plunge into cold running water, drain and return to the saucepan with the sugar and 1 cm/½ inch water. Simmer until soft, then add 1 tablespoon of cold water to stop cooking. Remove from the heat and reserve. Arrange the lettuce on 4 large plates and arrange the avocado, cucumber and mango slices over the lettuce.

3 Heat a wok or large frying pan, add the butter or oil and when hot, but not sizzling, add the lobster and stir-fry for 1–2 minutes or until heated through. Remove and drain on absorbent kitchen paper.

4 To make the dressing, heat the vegetable oil in a wok, then add the spring onions, ginger and garlic and stir-fry for 1 minute. Add the lime zest, lime juice, fish sauce, sugar and chilli sauce. Stir until the sugar dissolves. Remove from the heat, add the sesame oil with the orange rind and liquor.

5 Arrange the lobster meat over the salad and drizzle with dressing. Sprinkle with basil leaves, garnish with prawns and serve immediately.

DEEP-FRIED CRAB WONTONS

INGREDIENTS   Makes 24–30

2 tbsp sesame oil
6–8 water chestnuts, rinsed,
  drained and chopped
2 spring onions, peeled and
  finely chopped
1 cm/½ inch piece fresh root
  ginger, peeled and grated
185 g can white crabmeat,
  drained
50 ml/2 fl oz soy sauce
2 tbsp rice wine vinegar
½ tsp dried crushed chillies

2 tsp sugar
½ tsp hot pepper sauce, or to
  taste
1 tbsp freshly chopped
  coriander or dill
1 large egg yolk
1 packet wonton skins
vegetable oil for deep-frying
lime wedges, to garnish
dipping sauce, to serve
  (see page 52)

1 Heat a wok or large frying pan, add 1 tablespoon of the sesame oil and when hot, add the water chestnuts, spring onions and ginger and stir-fry for 1 minute. Remove from the heat and leave to cool slightly.

2 In a bowl, mix the crabmeat with the soy sauce, rice wine vinegar, crushed chillies, sugar, hot pepper sauce, chopped coriander or dill and the egg yolk. Stir in the cooled stir-fried mixture until well blended.

3 Lay the wonton skins on a work surface and place 1 teaspoonful of the crab mixture on the centre of each. Brush the edges of each wonton skin with a little water and fold up 1 corner to the opposite corner to form a triangle. Press to seal.

4 Bring the 2 corners of the triangle together to meet in the centre, brush 1 with a little water and overlap them, pressing to seal and form a 'tortellini' shape. Place on a baking sheet and continue with the remaining triangles.

5 Pour enough oil into a large wok to come 5 cm/2 inches up the sides and place over a high heat. Working in batches of 5 or 6, fry the wontons for 3 minutes, or until crisp and golden, turning once or twice.

6 Carefully remove the wontons with a slotted spoon, drain on absorbent kitchen paper and keep warm. Place on individual warmed serving plates, garnish each dish with a lime wedge and serve immediately with the Dipping Sauce.

SZECHUAN CHILLI PRAWNS

INGREDIENTS   Serves 4

450 g/1 lb raw tiger prawns
2 tbsp groundnut oil
1 onion, peeled and sliced
1 red pepper, deseeded and
   cut into strips
1 small red chilli, deseeded
   and thinly sliced
2 garlic cloves, peeled and
   finely chopped
2–3 spring onions, trimmed
   and diagonally sliced
freshly cooked rice or noodles,
   to serve

sprigs of fresh coriander or
   chilli flowers, to garnish

FOR THE CHILLI SAUCE:
1 tbsp cornflour
4 tbsp cold fish stock or water
2 tbsp soy sauce
2 tbsp sweet or hot chilli
   sauce, or to taste
2 tsp soft light brown sugar

1 Peel the prawns, leaving the tails attached if you like. Using a sharp knife, remove the black vein along the back of the prawns. Rinse and pat dry with absorbent kitchen paper.

2 Heat a wok or large frying pan, add the oil and when hot, add the onion, pepper and chilli and stir-fry for 4–5 minutes, or until the vegetables are tender but retain a bite. Stir in the garlic and cook for 30 seconds. Using a slotted spoon, transfer to a plate and reserve.

3 Add the prawns to the wok and stir-fry for 1–2 minutes, or until they turn pink and opaque.

4 Blend all the chilli sauce ingredients together in a bowl or jug, then stir into the prawns. Add the reserved vegetables and bring to the boil, stirring constantly. Cook for 1–2 minutes, or until the sauce is thickened and the prawns and vegetables are well coated.

5 Stir in the spring onions, tip on to a warmed platter and garnish with chilli flowers or coriander sprigs. Serve immediately with freshly cooked rice or noodles.

HELPFUL HINT

To make chilli flowers, cut off the tips of small chillies and remove the seeds. Snip the chilli to make 'petals', cutting to within 1 cm/½ inch of the stalk. Soak them in iced water for about 20 minutes.

STIR-FRIED SALMON WITH PEAS

INGREDIENTS   Serves 4

450 g/1 lb salmon fillet
salt
6 slices streaky bacon
1 tbsp vegetable oil
50 ml/2 fl oz chicken or fish
  stock
2 tbsp dark soy sauce
2 tbsp Chinese rice wine or
  dry sherry

1 tsp sugar
75 g/3 oz frozen peas, thawed
1–2 tbsp freshly shredded
  mint
1 tsp cornflour
sprigs of fresh mint, to garnish
freshly cooked noodles, to
  serve

1 Wipe and skin the salmon fillet and remove any pin bones. Slice into 2.5 cm/1 inch strips, place on a plate and sprinkle with salt. Leave for 20 minutes, then pat dry with absorbent kitchen paper and reserve.

2 Remove any cartilage from the bacon, cut into small dice and reserve.

3 Heat a wok or large frying pan over a high heat, then add the oil and when hot, add the bacon and stir-fry for 3 minutes or until crisp and golden. Push to one side and add the strips of salmon. Stir-fry gently for 2 minutes or until the flesh is opaque.

4 Pour the chicken or fish stock, soy sauce and Chinese rice wine or sherry into the wok, then stir in the sugar, peas and freshly shredded mint.

5 Blend the cornflour with 1 tablespoon of water to form a smooth paste and stir into the sauce. Bring to the boil, reduce the heat and simmer for 1 minute, or until slightly thickened and smooth. Garnish and serve immediately with noodles.

HELPFUL HINT

Sprinkling salmon with salt draws out some of the juices and makes the flesh firmer, so that it remains whole when cooked. Prior to cooking, pat the strips with absorbent kitchen paper to remove as much of the salty liquid as possible. Dark soy sauce is used in this recipe as it is slightly less salty than the light version. To reduce the salt content further, cook the noodles in plain boiling water without added salt.

CHINESE STEAMED SEA BASS WITH BLACK BEANS

INGREDIENTS   Serves 4

1.1 kg/2½ lb sea bass, cleaned
  with head and tail left on
1–2 tbsp rice wine or dry
  sherry
1½ tbsp groundnut oil
2–3 tbsp fermented black
  beans, rinsed and drained
1 garlic clove, peeled and
  finely chopped
1 cm/½ inch piece fresh root
  ginger, peeled and finely
  chopped

4 spring onions, trimmed and
  thinly sliced diagonally
2–3 tbsp soy sauce
125 ml/4 fl oz fish or chicken
  stock
1–2 tbsp sweet Chinese chilli
  sauce, or to taste
2 tsp sesame oil
sprigs of fresh coriander, to
  garnish

1 Using a sharp knife, cut 3–4 deep diagonal slashes along both sides of the fish. Sprinkle the Chinese rice wine or sherry inside and over the fish and gently rub into the skin on both sides.

2 Lightly brush a heatproof plate large enough to fit into a large wok or frying pan with a little of the groundnut oil. Place the fish on the plate, curving the fish along the inside edge of the dish, then leave for 20 minutes.

3 Place a wire rack or inverted ramekin in the wok and pour in enough water to come about 2.5 cm/1 inch up the side. Bring to the boil over a high heat.

4 Carefully place the plate with the fish on the rack or ramekin, cover and steam for 12–15 minutes, or until the fish is tender and the flesh is opaque when pierced with a knife near the bone.

5 Remove the plate with the fish from the wok and keep warm. Remove the rack or ramekin from the wok and pour off the water. Return the wok to the heat, add the remaining groundnut oil and swirl to coat the bottom and side. Add the black beans, garlic and ginger and stir-fry for 1 minute.

6 Add the spring onions, soy sauce, fish or chicken stock and boil for 1 minute. Stir in the chilli sauce and sesame oil, then pour the sauce over the cooked fish. Garnish with coriander sprigs and serve immediately.

SWEET-&-SOUR FISH

INGREDIENTS
Serves 4

125 g/4 oz carrot, peeled and
  cut into julienne strips
125 g/4 oz red or green pepper
125 g/4 oz mangetout, cut in
  half diagonally
125 g/4 oz frozen peas, thawed
2–3 spring onions, trimmed
  and sliced diagonally into
  5 cm/2 inch pieces
450 g/1 lb small thin skinless
  plaice fillets
1½–2 tbsp cornflour
vegetable oil for frying
sprigs of fresh coriander,
  to garnish

**FOR THE SWEET-&-SOUR
  SAUCE:**
2 tsp cornflour
300 ml/½ pint fish or chicken
  stock
4 cm/1½ inch piece fresh root
  ginger, peeled and finely
  sliced
2 tbsp soy sauce
2 tbsp rice wine vinegar or dry
  sherry
2 tbsp tomato ketchup or
  tomato concentrate
2 tbsp Chinese rice vinegar or
  cider vinegar
1½ tbsp soft light brown sugar

1 Make the sauce. Place the cornflour in a saucepan and gradually whisk in the stock. Stir in the remaining sauce ingredients and bring to the boil, stirring, until the sauce thickens. Simmer for 2 minutes, then remove from the heat and reserve.

2 Bring a saucepan of water to the boil. Add the carrot, return to the boil and cook for 3 minutes. Add the pepper and cook for 1 minute. Add the mange-tout and peas and cook for 30 seconds. Drain, rinse under cold running water and drain again, then add to the sweet and sour sauce with the spring onions.

3 Using a sharp knife, make crisscross slashes across the top of each fish fillet then lightly coat on both sides with the cornflour.

4 Pour enough oil into a large wok to come 5 cm/2 inches up the side. Heat to 190°C/375°F, or until a cube of bread browns in 30 seconds. Fry the fish fillets, 2 at a time, for 3–5 minutes, or until crisp and golden, turning once. Using a fish slice, remove and drain on absorbent kitchen paper. Keep warm.

5 Bring the sweet and sour sauce to the boil, stirring constantly. Arrange the fish fillets on a warmed platter and pour over the hot sauce. Garnish with sprigs of coriander and serve immediately.

FISH BALLS IN HOT YELLOW BEAN SAUCE

INGREDIENTS   Serves 4

450 g/1 lb skinless white fish
  fillets, such as cod or
  haddock, cut into pieces
½ tsp salt
1 tbsp cornflour
2 spring onions, trimmed and
  chopped
1 tbsp freshly chopped
  coriander
1 tsp soy sauce
1 medium egg white
freshly ground black pepper
sprig of tarragon, to garnish
freshly cooked rice, to serve

**FOR THE YELLOW BEAN
  SAUCE:**
75 ml/3 fl oz fish or chicken
  stock
1–2 tsp yellow bean sauce
2 tbsp soy sauce
1–2 tbsp Chinese rice wine or
  dry sherry
1 tsp chilli bean sauce, or to
  taste
1 tsp sesame oil
1 tsp sugar (optional)

1 Put the fish pieces, salt, cornflour, spring onions, coriander, soy sauce and egg white into a food processor, season to taste with pepper, then blend until a smooth paste forms, scraping down the sides of the bowl occasionally.

2 With dampened hands, shape the mixture into 2.5 cm/1 inch balls. Transfer to a baking tray and chill in the refrigerator for at least 30 minutes.

3 Bring a large saucepan of water to simmering point. Working in 2 or 3 batches, drop in the fish balls and poach gently for 3–4 minutes or until they float to the top. Transfer to absorbent kitchen paper to drain.

4 Put all the sauce ingredients in a wok or large frying pan and bring to the boil. Add the fish balls to the sauce and stir-fry gently for 2–3 minutes until piping hot. Transfer to a warmed serving dish, garnish with sprigs of tarragon and serve immediately with freshly cooked rice.

FOOD FACT

Yellow bean and brown bean sauces are made from fermented soy beans and have a strong salty taste. If you buy yellow bean sauce in a can, transfer it to a glass container and store in the refrigerator; it will keep for up to a year.

STEAMED WHOLE TROUT WITH GINGER & SPRING ONION

INGREDIENTS   Serves 4

2 x 450–700 g/1–1½ lb whole
  trout, gutted with heads
  removed
coarse sea salt
2 tbsp groundnut oil
½ tbsp soy sauce
1 tbsp sesame oil
2 garlic cloves, peeled and
  thinly sliced
2.5 cm/1 inch piece fresh root
  ginger, peeled and thinly
  slivered

2 spring onions, trimmed and
  thinly sliced diagonally

TO GARNISH:
chive leaves
lemon slices

TO SERVE:
freshly cooked rice
Oriental salad, to serve

1 Wipe the fish inside and out with absorbent kitchen paper then rub with salt inside and out and leave for about 20 minutes. Pat dry with absorbent kitchen paper.

2 Set a steamer rack or inverted ramekin in a large wok and pour in enough water to come about 5 cm/2 inches up the side of the wok. Bring to the boil.

3 Brush a heatproof dinner plate with a little of the groundnut oil and place the fish on the plate with the tails pointing in opposite directions. Place the plate on the rack, cover tightly and simmer over a medium heat for 10–12 minutes, or until tender and the flesh is opaque near the bone.

4 Carefully transfer the plate to a heatproof surface. Sprinkle with the soy sauce and keep warm.

5 Pour the water out of the wok and return to the heat. Add the remaining groundnut and sesame oils and when hot, add the garlic, ginger and spring onion and stir-fry for 2 minutes, or until golden. Pour over the fish, garnish with chive leaves and lemon slices and serve immediately with rice and an Oriental salad.

FOOD FACT

There are 3 types of trout: rainbow trout, golden trout and brown trout.

STIR-FRIED SQUID WITH ASPARAGUS

INGREDIENTS
Serves 4

450 g/1 lb squid, cleaned and cut into 1 cm/½ inch rings

225 g/8 oz fresh asparagus, sliced diagonally into 6.5 cm/2½ inch pieces

2 tbsp groundnut oil

2 garlic cloves, peeled and thinly sliced

2.5 cm/1 inch piece fresh root ginger, peeled and thinly sliced

225 g/8 oz pak choi, trimmed

75 ml/3 fl oz chicken stock

2 tbsp soy sauce

2 tbsp oyster sauce

1 tbsp Chinese rice wine or dry sherry

2 tsp cornflour, blended with 1 tbsp water

1 tbsp sesame oil

1 tbsp toasted sesame seeds

freshly cooked rice, to serve

1 Bring a medium saucepan of water to the boil over a high heat. Add the squid, return to the boil and cook for 30 seconds. Using a wide wok strainer or slotted spoon, transfer to a colander, drain and reserve.

2 Add the asparagus pieces to the boiling water and blanch for 2 minutes. Drain and reserve.

3 Heat a wok or large frying pan, add the groundnut oil and when hot, add the garlic and ginger and stir-fry for 30 seconds. Add the pak choi, stir-fry for 1–2 minutes, then pour in the stock and cook for 1 minute.

4 Blend the soy sauce, oyster sauce and Chinese rice wine or sherry in a bowl or jug, then pour into the wok.

5 Add the reserved squid and asparagus to the wok and stir-fry for 1 minute. Stir the blended cornflour into the wok. Stir-fry for 1 minute, or until the sauce thickens and all the ingredients are well coated.

6 Stir in the sesame oil, give a final stir and turn into a warmed serving dish. Sprinkle with the toasted sesame seeds and serve immediately with freshly cooked rice.

TASTY TIP

Pak choi is a member of the cabbage family. If available, use baby pak choi for this recipe or Shanghai pak choi, which is slightly smaller and more delicately flavoured.

CHINESE FIVE SPICE MARINATED SALMON

INGREDIENTS Serves 4

700 g/1½ lb skinless salmon fillet, cut into 2.5 cm/1 inch strips
2 medium egg whites
1 tbsp cornflour
vegetable oil for frying
4 spring onions, cut diagonally into 5 cm/2 inch pieces
125 ml/4 fl oz fish stock
lime or lemon wedges, to garnish

FOR THE MARINADE:
3 tbsp soy sauce
3 tbsp Chinese rice wine or dry sherry
2 tsp sesame oil
1 tbsp soft brown sugar
1 tbsp lime or lemon juice
1 tsp Chinese five spice powder
2–3 dashes hot pepper sauce

1 Combine the marinade ingredients in a shallow nonmetallic baking dish until well blended. Add the salmon strips and stir gently to coat. Leave to marinate in the refrigerator for 20–30 minutes.

2 Using a slotted spoon or fish slice, remove the salmon pieces, drain on absorbent kitchen paper and pat dry. Reserve the marinade.

3 Beat the egg whites with the cornflour to make a batter. Add the salmon strips and stir into the batter until coated completely.

4 Pour enough oil into a large wok to come 5 cm/2 inches up the side and place over a high heat. Working in 2 or 3 batches, add the salmon strips and cook for 1–2 minutes or until golden. Remove from the wok with a slotted spoon and drain on absorbent kitchen paper. Reserve.

5 Discard the hot oil and wipe the wok clean. Add the marinade, spring onions and stock to the wok. Bring to the boil and simmer for 1 minute. Add the salmon strips and stir-fry gently until coated in the sauce. Spoon into a warmed shallow serving dish, garnish with the lime or lemon wedges and serve immediately.

HELPFUL HINT

If liked, marinate the salmon for 4–6 hours for a stronger and more intense flavour.

SCALLOPS WITH BLACK BEAN SAUCE

INGREDIENTS — Serves 4

700 g/1½ lb scallops, with their coral
2 tbsp vegetable oil
2–3 tbsp Chinese fermented black beans, rinsed, drained and coarsely chopped
2 garlic cloves, peeled and finely chopped
4 cm/1½ inch piece fresh root ginger, peeled and finely chopped
4–5 spring onions, thinly sliced diagonally
2–3 tbsp soy sauce
1½ tbsp Chinese rice wine or dry sherry
1–2 tsp sugar
1 tbsp fish stock or water
2–3 dashes hot pepper sauce
1 tbsp sesame oil
freshly cooked noodles, to serve

1 Pat the scallops dry with absorbent kitchen paper. Carefully separate the orange coral from the scallop. Peel off and discard the membrane and thickish opaque muscle that attaches the coral to the scallop. Cut any large scallops crossways in half, leave the corals whole.

2 Heat a wok or large frying pan, add the oil and when hot, add the white scallop meat and stir-fry for 2 minutes, or until just beginning to colour on the edges. Using a slotted spoon or spatula, transfer to a plate. Reserve.

3 Add the black beans, garlic and ginger and stir-fry for 1 minute. Add the spring onions, soy sauce, Chinese rice wine or sherry, sugar, fish stock or water, hot pepper sauce and the corals and stir until mixed.

4 Return the scallops and juices to the wok and stir-fry gently for 3 minutes, or until the scallops and corals are cooked through. Add a little more stock or water if necessary. Stir in the sesame oil and turn into a heated serving dish. Serve immediately with noodles.

FOOD FACT

Fermented black beans are also known as salted black beans or simply black beans. These small black soybeans need rinsing only briefly, then should be crushed or coarsely chopped to release their tangy flavour and aroma.

PORK FRIED NOODLES

INGREDIENTS Serves 4

125 g/4 oz dried thread egg noodles

125 g/4 oz broccoli florets

4 tbsp groundnut oil

350 g/12 oz pork tenderloin, cut into slices

3 tbsp soy sauce

1 tbsp lemon juice

pinch of sugar

1 tsp chilli sauce

1 tbsp sesame oil

2.5 cm/1 inch piece fresh root ginger, peeled and cut into sticks

1 garlic clove, peeled and chopped

1 green chilli, deseeded and sliced

125 g/4 oz mangetout, halved

2 medium eggs, lightly beaten

227 g can water chestnuts, drained and sliced

TO GARNISH:

radish rose

spring onion tassels

1 Place the noodles in a bowl and cover with boiling water. Leave to stand for 20 minutes, stirring occasionally, or until tender. Drain and reserve. Meanwhile, blanch the broccoli in a saucepan of lightly salted boiling water for 2 minutes. Drain, refresh under cold running water and reserve.

2 Heat a large wok or frying pan, add the groundnut oil and heat until just smoking. Add the pork and stir-fry for 5 minutes, or until browned. Using a slotted spoon, remove the pork slices and reserve.

3 Mix together the soy sauce, lemon juice, sugar, chilli sauce and sesame oil and reserve.

4 Add the ginger to the wok and stir-fry for 30 seconds. Add the garlic and chilli and stir-fry for 30 seconds. Add the reserved broccoli and stir-fry for 3 minutes. Stir in the mangetout, pork and reserved noodles with the beaten eggs and water chestnuts and stir-fry for 5 minutes or until heated through. Pour over the reserved chilli sauce, toss well and turn into a warmed serving dish. Garnish and serve immediately.

FOOD FACT

Make radish roses by topping and tailing the radish. Make small slits from the top to the base, then plunge the radish into iced water for 30 minutes until petals form.

HOISIN PORK

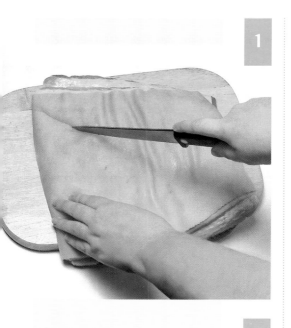

INGREDIENTS	Serves 4

1.4 kg/3 lb piece lean belly pork, boned
sea salt
2 tsp Chinese five spice powder
2 garlic cloves, peeled and chopped

1 tsp sesame oil
4 tbsp hoisin sauce
1 tbsp clear honey
assorted salad leaves, to garnish

1 Preheat the oven to 200°C/400°F/Gas Mark 6, 15 minutes before cooking. Using a sharp knife, cut the pork skin in a crisscross pattern, making sure not to cut all the way through into the flesh. Rub the salt evenly over the skin and leave to stand for 30 minutes.

2 Meanwhile, mix together the five spice powder, garlic, sesame oil, hoisin sauce and honey until smooth. Rub the mixture evenly over the pork skin. Place the pork on a plate and chill in the refrigerator to marinate for up to 6 hours.

3 Place the pork on a wire rack set inside a roasting tin and roast the pork in the preheated oven for 1–1¼ hours, or until the pork is very crisp and the juices run clear when pierced with a skewer.

4 Remove the pork from the heat, leave to rest for 15 minutes, then cut into strips.

Arrange on a warmed serving platter. Garnish with salad leaves and serve immediately.

FOOD FACT

Belly of pork, also known as streaky pork, is a thin cut of meat and with roughly the same proportion of fat to lean meat in thin alternate layers. Here, it is well cooked so that the meat is tender and the fat golden brown and crispy. Pork is the most popular meat of China and in rural parts nearly every family will keep a pig, which thrives on kitchen scraps.

COCONUT BEEF

INGREDIENTS
Serves 4

450 g/1 lb beef rump or sirloin
  steak
4 tbsp groundnut oil
2 bunches spring onions,
  trimmed and thickly sliced
1 red chilli, deseeded and
  chopped
1 garlic clove, peeled and
  chopped

2 cm/1 inch piece fresh root
  ginger, peeled and cut into
  matchsticks
125 g/4 oz shiitake mushrooms
200 ml/7 fl oz coconut cream
150 ml/¼ pint chicken stock
4 tbsp freshly chopped
  coriander
salt and freshly ground black
  pepper
freshly cooked rice, to serve

1 Trim off any fat or gristle from the beef and cut into thin strips. Heat a wok or large frying pan, add 2 tablespoons of the oil and heat until just smoking. Add the beef and cook for 5–8 minutes, turning occasionally, until browned on all sides. Using a slotted spoon, transfer the beef to a plate and keep warm.

2 Add the remaining oil to the wok and heat until almost smoking. Add the spring onions, chilli, garlic and ginger and cook for 1 minute, stirring occasionally. Add the mushrooms and stir-fry for 3 minutes. Using a slotted spoon, transfer the mushroom mixture to a plate and keep warm.

3 Return the beef to the wok, pour in the coconut cream and stock. Bring to the boil and simmer for 3–4 minutes, or until the juices are slightly reduced and the beef is just tender.

4 Return the mushroom mixture to the wok and heat through. Stir in the chopped coriander and season to taste with salt and pepper. Serve immediately with freshly cooked rice.

FOOD FACT

Shiitake mushrooms, which grow naturally on decaying trees are now cultivated on the *shii* tree, hence their name. Here they are used fresh, but are often used dried. To prepare fresh mushrooms, wipe with damp absorbent kitchen paper, remove and discard the tough stalks and slice the caps, if large.

PORK MEATBALLS WITH VEGETABLES

INGREDIENTS   Serves 4

450 g/1 lb pork mince
2 tbsp freshly chopped
  coriander
2 garlic cloves, peeled and
  chopped
1 tbsp light soy sauce
salt and freshly ground black
  pepper
2 tbsp groundnut oil
2 cm/1 inch piece fresh root
  ginger, peeled and cut into
  matchsticks
1 red pepper, deseeded and
  cut into chunks

1 green pepper, deseeded and
  cut into chunks
2 courgettes, trimmed and cut
  into sticks
125 g/4 oz baby sweetcorn,
  halved lengthways
3 tbsp light soy sauce
1 tsp sesame oil
fresh coriander leaves, to
  garnish
freshly cooked noodles, to
  serve

1 Mix together the pork mince, the chopped coriander, half the garlic and the soy sauce, then season to taste with salt and pepper. Divide into 20 portions and roll into balls. Place on a baking sheet, cover with clingfilm and chill in the refrigerator for at least 30 minutes.

2 Heat a wok or large frying pan, add the groundnut oil and when hot, add the meatballs and cook for 8–10 minutes, or until the pork balls are browned all over, turning occasionally. Using a slotted spoon, transfer the balls to a plate and keep warm.

3 Add the ginger and remaining garlic to the wok and stir-fry for 30 seconds. Add the red and green peppers and stir-fry for 5 minutes. Add the courgettes and sweetcorn and stir-fry for 3 minutes.

4 Return the pork balls to the wok, add the soy sauce and sesame oil and stir-fry for 1 minute, until heated through. Garnish with coriander leaves and serve immediately on a bed of noodles.

HELPFUL HINT

Chilling the meatballs firms and helps prevent them breaking up during cooking. If you find it easier, cook the pork balls in 2 batches.

SPICY PORK

INGREDIENTS   Serves 4

4 tbsp groundnut oil

2.5 cm/1 inch piece fresh root ginger, peeled and cut into matchsticks

1 garlic clove, peeled and chopped

2 medium carrots, peeled and cut into matchsticks

1 medium aubergine, trimmed and cubed

700 g/1½ lb pork fillet, thickly sliced

400 ml/14 fl oz coconut milk

2 tbsp Thai red curry paste

4 tbsp Thai fish sauce

2 tsp caster sugar

227 g can bamboo shoots in brine, drained and cut into matchsticks

salt, to taste

lime zest, to garnish

freshly cooked rice, to serve

1 Heat a wok or large frying pan, add 2 tablespoons of the oil and when hot, add the ginger, garlic, carrots and aubergine and stir-fry for 3 minutes. Using a slotted spoon, transfer to a plate and keep warm.

2 Add the remaining oil to the wok, heat until smoking, then add the pork and stir-fry for 5–8 minutes or until browned all over. Transfer to a plate and keep warm. Wipe the wok clean.

3 Pour half the coconut milk into the wok, stir in the red curry paste and bring to the boil. Boil rapidly for 4 minutes, stirring occasionally, or until the sauce is reduced by half.

4 Add the fish sauce and sugar to the wok and bring back to the boil. Return the pork and vegetables to the wok with the

bamboo shoots. Return to the boil, then simmer for 4 minutes.

5 Stir in the remaining coconut milk and season to taste with salt. Simmer for 2 minutes or until heated through. Garnish with lime zest and serve immediately with rice.

FOOD FACT

Coconut milk is the thick sweet liquid produced by pouring boiling water over grated coconut, then squeezing it out. Using twice as much water by volume as grated coconut produces 'milk' of normal thickness. Using equal quantities produces 'cream', but this is not the same as commercial coconut cream.

PORK WITH TOFU & COCONUT

INGREDIENTS   Serves 4

50 g/2 oz unsalted cashew nuts
1 tbsp ground coriander
1 tbsp ground cumin
2 tsp hot chilli powder
2.5 cm/1 inch piece fresh root ginger, peeled and chopped
1 tbsp oyster sauce
4 tbsp groundnut oil
400 ml/14 fl oz coconut milk
175 g/6 oz rice noodles
450 g/1 lb pork tenderloin, thickly sliced

1 red chilli, deseeded and sliced
1 green chilli, deseeded and sliced
1 bunch spring onions, trimmed and thickly sliced
3 tomatoes, roughly chopped
75 g/3 oz tofu, drained
2 tbsp freshly chopped coriander
2 tbsp freshly chopped mint
salt and freshly ground black pepper

1 Place the cashew nuts, coriander, cumin, chilli powder, ginger and oyster sauce in a food processor and blend until well ground. Heat a wok or large frying pan, add 2 tablespoons of the oil and when hot, add the cashew mixture and stir-fry for 1 minute. Stir in the coconut milk, bring to the boil, then simmer for 1 minute. Pour into a small jug and reserve. Wipe the wok clean.

2 Meanwhile, place the rice noodles in a bowl, cover with boiling water, leave to stand for 5 minutes, then drain thoroughly.

3 Reheat the wok, add the remaining oil and when hot, add the pork and stir-fry for 5 minutes or until browned all over. Add the chillies and spring onions and stir-fry for 2 minutes.

4 Add the tomatoes and tofu to the wok with the noodles and coconut mixture and stir-fry for a further 2 minutes, or until heated through, being careful not to break up the tofu. Sprinkle with the chopped coriander and mint, season to taste with salt and pepper and stir. Tip into a warmed serving dish and serve immediately.

HELPFUL HINT

Dried rice noodles are white and opaque and come in a variety of shapes. Most types need to be soaked briefly in boiling water before use, but always check the packet instructions as soaking times may vary.

CHILLI BEEF

INGREDIENTS   Serves 4

550 g/1¼ lb beef rump steak
2 tbsp groundnut oil
2 carrots, peeled and cut into
  matchsticks
125 g/4 oz mangetout,
  shredded
125 g/4 oz beansprouts
1 green chilli, deseeded and
  chopped

2 tbsp sesame seeds
freshly cooked rice, to serve

FOR THE MARINADE:
1 garlic clove, peeled and
  chopped
3 tbsp soy sauce
1 tbsp sweet chilli sauce
4 tbsp groundnut oil

1 Using a sharp knife, trim the beef, discarding any fat or gristle, then cut into thin strips and place in a shallow dish. Combine all the marinade ingredients in a bowl and pour over the beef. Turn the beef in the marinade until coated evenly, cover with clingfilm and leave to marinate in the refrigerator for at least 30 minutes.

2 Heat a wok or large frying pan, add the groundnut oil and heat until almost smoking, then add the carrots and stir-fry for 3–4 minutes, or until softened. Add the mangetout and stir-fry for a further 1 minute. Using a slotted spoon, transfer the vegetables to a plate and keep warm.

3 Lift the beef strips from the marinade, shaking to remove excess marinade. Reserve the marinade. Add the beef to the wok and stir-fry for 3 minutes or until browned all over.

4 Return the stir-fried vegetables to the wok together with the beansprouts, chilli and sesame seeds and cook for 1 minute. Stir in the reserved marinade and stir-fry for 1–2 minutes or until heated through. Tip into a warmed serving dish or spoon on to individual plates and serve immediately with freshly cooked rice.

FOOD FACT

Chillies have become a favourite Chinese ingredient, especially in Szechuan. Chilli sauce is a mixture of crushed fresh chillies, plums, vinegar and salt. It is available in several varieties: extra hot, hot or sweet, as used here, which is the mildest version. Chilli sauce may be used as a marinade or as a dip.

PORK WITH BLACK BEAN SAUCE

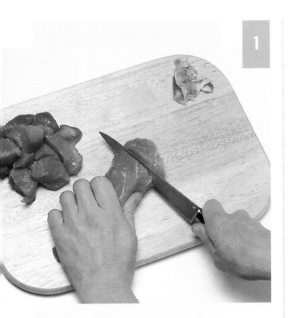

INGREDIENTS   Serves 4

700 g/1½ lb pork tenderloin
4 tbsp light soy sauce
2 tbsp groundnut oil
1 garlic clove, peeled and
    chopped
2.5 cm/1 inch piece fresh root
    ginger, peeled and cut into
    matchsticks
1 large carrot, peeled and
    sliced

1 red pepper, deseeded and
    sliced
1 green pepper, deseeded and
    sliced
160 g jar black bean sauce
salt
snipped fresh chives, to
    garnish
freshly steamed rice, to serve

1 Using a sharp knife, trim the pork, discarding any fat or sinew and cut into bite-sized chunks. Place in a large shallow dish and spoon over the soy sauce. Turn to coat evenly, cover with clingfilm and leave to marinate for at least 30 minutes. When in the refrigerator ready to use, lift the pork from the marinade, shaking off as much marinade as possible, and pat dry with absorbent kitchen paper. Reserve the marinade.

2 Heat a wok, add the groundnut oil and when hot, add the chopped garlic and ginger and stir-fry for 30 seconds. Add the carrot and the red and green peppers and stir-fry for 3–4 minutes or until just softened.

3 Add the pork to the wok and stir-fry for 5–7 minutes, or until browned all over and tender. Pour in the reserved marinade and black bean sauce. Bring to

the boil, stirring constantly until well blended, then simmer for 1 minute, until heated through thoroughly. Tip into a warmed serving dish or spoon on to individual plates. Garnish with snipped chives and serve immediately with steamed rice.

TASTY TIP

Before cooking the pork, shake off as much marinade as possible, then pat the meat dry with absorbent kitchen paper. This will ensure that the meat is fried in the hot oil and browns properly. If too much liquid is added with the meat, it tends to steam in the juices.

PORK SPRING ROLLS

INGREDIENTS

Serves 4

125 g/4 oz pork tenderloin
2 tbsp light soy sauce
225 ml/8 fl oz groundnut oil
1 medium carrot, peeled and
  cut into matchsticks
75 g/3 oz button mushrooms,
  wiped and sliced
4 spring onions, trimmed and
  thinly sliced

75 g/3 oz beansprouts
1 garlic clove, peeled and
  chopped
1 tbsp dark soy sauce
12 large sheets filo pastry
  folded in half
spring onion curls, to garnish
Chinese-style dipping sauce,
  to serve

1 Trim the pork, discarding any sinew or fat, and cut into very fine strips. Place in a small bowl, pour over the light soy sauce and stir until well coated. Cover with clingfilm and leave to marinate in the refrigerator for at least 30 minutes.

2 Heat a wok or large frying pan, add 1 tablespoon of the oil and when hot, add the carrot and mushrooms and stir-fry for 3 minutes or until softened. Add the spring onions, beansprouts and garlic, stir-fry for 2 minutes, then transfer the vegetables to a bowl and reserve.

3 Drain the pork well, add to the wok and stir-fry for 2–4 minutes or until browned. Add the pork to the vegetables and leave to cool. Stir in the dark soy sauce and mix the filling well.

4 Lay the folded filo pastry sheets on a work surface. Divide the filling between the sheets, placing it at one end. Brush the filo edges with water, then fold the sides over and roll up.

5 Heat the remaining oil in a large wok to 180°C/350°F and cook the spring rolls in batches for 2–3 minutes, or until golden, turning the rolls during cooking. Using a slotted spoon, remove and drain on absorbent kitchen paper. Garnish with spring onion curls and serve immediately with a Chinese-style dipping sauce.

TASTY TIP

To make a dipping sauce, blend together 2 tablespoons dark soy sauce, 1 tablespoon Chinese rice wine or dry sherry, 2 teaspoons chilli bean sauce, 2 teaspoons toasted sesame seed oil and 1 teaspoon caster sugar. Stir in 1 very finely chopped spring onion.

SPECIAL FRIED RICE

INGREDIENTS   Serves 4

25 g/1 oz butter
4 medium eggs, beaten
4 tbsp vegetable oil
1 bunch spring onions,
  trimmed and shredded
225 g/8 oz cooked ham, diced
125 g/4 oz large cooked
  prawns with tails left on
75 g/3 oz peas, thawed if
  frozen

200 g can water chestnuts,
  drained and roughly
  chopped
450 g/1 lb cooked long-grain
  rice
3 tbsp dark soy sauce
1 tbsp dry sherry
2 tbsp freshly chopped
  coriander
salt and freshly ground black
  pepper

1 Melt the butter in a wok or large frying pan and pour in half the beaten egg. Cook for 4 minutes drawing the edges of the omelette in to allow the uncooked egg to set into a round shape. Using a fish slice, lift the omelette from the wok and roll into a sausage shape. Leave to cool completely then using a sharp knife slice the omelette into rings.

2 Wipe the wok with absorbent kitchen paper and return to the heat. Add the oil and when hot, add the spring onions, ham, prawns, peas and chopped water chestnuts and stir-fry for 2 minutes. Add the rice and stir-fry for a further 3 minutes.

3 Add the remaining beaten eggs and stir-fry for 3 minutes, or until the egg has scrambled and set. Stir in the soy sauce, sherry and chopped coriander. Season to taste with salt and pepper and heat through thoroughly. Add the omelette rings and gently stir without breaking up the egg too much. Serve immediately.

HELPFUL HINT

In Chinese cuisine, rice is always cooked by the absorption method, rather than in large quantities of boiling water, so that all the flavour and nutrients are retained. Long-grain rice is popular, but Thai fragrant rice is served on special occasions. Medium and short-grain rices are also used in savoury dishes. Long-grain rice absorbs 1½ to 3 times its volume in water, so you will need to start with about 175 g/6 oz uncooked rice for this dish.

BEEF & BABY CORN STIR FRY

INGREDIENTS   Serves 4

3 tbsp light soy sauce

1 tbsp clear honey, warmed

450 g/1 lb beef rump steak, trimmed and thinly sliced

6 tbsp groundnut oil

125 g/4 oz shiitake mushrooms, wiped and halved

125 g/4 oz beansprouts, rinsed

2.5 cm/1 inch piece fresh root ginger, peeled and cut into matchsticks

125 g/4 oz mangetout, halved lengthways

125 g/4 oz broccoli, trimmed and cut into florets

1 medium carrot, peeled and cut into matchsticks

125 g/4 oz baby sweetcorn cobs, halved lengthways

¼ head Chinese leaves, shredded

1 tbsp chilli sauce

3 tbsp black bean sauce

1 tbsp dry sherry

freshly cooked noodles, to serve

1 Mix together the soy sauce and honey in a shallow dish. Add the sliced beef and turn to coat evenly. Cover with clingfilm and leave to marinate for at least 30 minutes, turning occasionally.

2 Heat a wok or large frying pan, add 2 tablespoons of the oil and heat until just smoking. Add the mushrooms and stir-fry for 1 minute. Add the bean sprouts and stir-fry for 1 minute. Using a slotted spoon, transfer the mushroom mixture to a plate and keep warm.

3 Drain the beef, reserving the marinade. Reheat the wok, pour in 2 tablespoons of the oil and heat until smoking. Add the beef and stir-fry for 4 minutes or until browned. Transfer to a plate and keep warm.

4 Add the remaining oil to the wok and heat until just smoking. Add the ginger, mangetout, broccoli, carrot and the baby sweetcorn with the shredded Chinese leaves and stir-fry for 3 minutes. Stir in the chilli and black bean sauces, the sherry, the reserved marinade and the beef and mushroom mixture. Stir-fry for 2 minutes, then serve immediately with freshly cooked noodles.

TASTY TIP

You could use lean pork, such as fillet, or skinned, boneless chicken breasts instead of rump steak, if you prefer. For a vegetarian version, use cubed smoked tofu.

SWEET-&-SOUR SPARERIBS

INGREDIENTS   Serves 4

1.6 kg/3½ lb pork spareribs
4 tbsp clear honey
1 tbsp Worcestershire sauce
1 tsp Chinese five spice powder
4 tbsp soy sauce
2½ tbsp dry sherry
1 tsp chilli sauce

2 garlic cloves, peeled and
  chopped
1½ tbsp tomato purée
1 tsp dry mustard powder
  (optional)
spring onion curls, to garnish

1 Preheat the oven to 200°C/ 400°F/Gas Mark 6, 15 minutes before cooking. If necessary, place the ribs on a chopping board and using a sharp knife, cut the joint in between the ribs, to form single ribs. Place the ribs in a shallow dish in a single layer.

2 Spoon the honey, the Worcestershire sauce, Chinese five spice powder with the soy sauce, sherry and chilli sauce into a small saucepan and heat gently, stirring until smooth. Stir in the chopped garlic, the tomato purée and mustard powder, if using.

3 Pour the honey mixture over ribs and spoon over until the ribs are coated evenly. Cover with clingfilm and leave to marinate overnight in the refrigerator, occasionally spooning the marinade over the ribs.

4 When ready to cook, remove the ribs from the marinade and place in a shallow roasting tin. Spoon over a little of the marinade and reserve the remainder. Place the spareribs in the preheated oven and cook for 35–40 minutes, or until cooked and the outsides are crisp. Baste occasionally with the reserved marinade during cooking. Garnish with a few spring onion curls and serve immediately, either as a starter or as a meat accompaniment.

TASTY TIP

Marinating spareribs overnight not only flavours the meat, but makes it wonderfully tender as well. If you do not have enough time for this, place the ribs in a saucepan and pour in enough water to just cover. Add 1 tablespoon of wine vinegar, bring to the boil, then simmer gently for 15 minutes. Drain well, toss in the marinade and roast straight away, basting occasionally as before.

LAMB WITH STIR-FRIED VEGETABLES

INGREDIENTS   Serves 4

550 g/1¼ lb lamb fillet, cut into strips

2.5 cm/1 inch piece fresh root ginger, peeled and cut into matchsticks

2 garlic cloves, peeled and chopped

4 tbsp soy sauce

2 tbsp dry sherry

2 tsp cornflour

4 tbsp groundnut oil

75 g/3 oz French beans, trimmed and cut in half

2 medium carrots, peeled and cut into matchsticks

1 red pepper, deseeded and cut into chunks

1 yellow pepper, deseeded and cut into chunks

225 g can water chestnuts, drained and halved

3 tomatoes, chopped

freshly cooked sticky rice in banana leaves, to serve (optional)

1 Place the lamb strips in a shallow dish. Mix together the ginger and half the garlic in a small bowl. Pour over the soy sauce and sherry and stir well. Pour over the lamb and stir until coated lightly. Cover with clingfilm and leave to marinate for at least 30 minutes, occasionally spooning the marinade over the lamb.

2 Using a slotted spoon, lift the lamb from the marinade and place on a plate. Blend the cornflour and the marinade together until smooth and reserve.

3 Heat a wok or large frying pan, add 2 tablespoons of the oil and when hot, add the remaining garlic, French beans, carrots and peppers and stir-fry

for 5 minutes. Using a slotted spoon, transfer the vegetables to a plate and keep warm.

4 Heat the remaining oil in the wok, add the lamb and stir-fry for 2 minutes or until tender. Return the vegetables to the wok with the water chestnuts, tomatoes and reserved marinade mixture. Bring to the boil then simmer for 1 minute. Serve immediately with freshly cooked sticky rice in banana leaves, if liked.

FOOD FACT

Sticky or glutinous rice has a high starch content. The grains stick together when cooked, making it easy to eat with chopsticks.

SZECHUAN BEEF

INGREDIENTS   Serves 4

450 g/1 lb beef fillet
3 tbsp hoisin sauce
2 tbsp yellow bean sauce
2 tbsp dry sherry
1 tbsp brandy
2 tbsp groundnut oil
2 red chillies, deseeded and
  sliced
8 bunches spring onions,
  trimmed and chopped
2 garlic cloves, peeled and
  chopped
2.5 cm/1 inch piece fresh root
  ginger, peeled and cut into
  matchsticks

1 carrot, peeled, sliced
  lengthways and cut into
  short lengths
2 green peppers, deseeded and
  cut into 2.5 cm/1 inch pieces
227 g can water chestnuts,
  drained and halved
sprigs of fresh coriander, to
  garnish
freshly cooked noodles with
  freshly ground Szechuan
  peppercorns, to serve

1 Trim the beef, discarding any sinew or fat, then cut into 5 mm/¼ inch strips. Place in a large shallow dish. In a bowl, stir the hoisin sauce, yellow bean sauce, sherry and brandy together until well blended. Pour over the beef and turn until coated evenly. Cover with clingfilm and leave to marinate for at least 30 minutes.

2 Heat a wok or large frying pan, add the oil and when hot, add the chillies, spring onions, garlic and ginger and stir-fry for 2 minutes or until softened. Using a slotted spoon, transfer to a plate and keep warm.

3 Add the carrot and peppers to the wok and stir-fry for 4 minutes or until slightly softened. Transfer to a plate and keep warm.

4 Drain the beef, reserving the marinade, add to the wok and stir-fry for 3–5 minutes or until browned. Return the chilli mixture, the carrot and pepper mixture and the marinade to the wok, add the water chestnuts and stir-fry for 2 minutes or until heated through. Garnish with sprigs of coriander and serve immediately with the noodles.

FOOD FACT

Water chestnuts grow on a reed-like plant. When peeled, they are white, sweet and crunchy and it is their texture rather than flavour that makes them such a popular addition to stir fries.

CASHEW & PORK STIR FRY

INGREDIENTS   Serves 4

450 g/1 lb pork tenderloin
4 tbsp soy sauce
1 tbsp cornflour
125 g/4 oz unsalted cashew
nuts
4 tbsp sunflower oil
450 g/1 lb leeks, trimmed and
shredded
2.5 cm/1 inch piece fresh root
ginger, peeled and cut into
matchsticks

2 garlic cloves, peeled and
chopped
1 red pepper, deseeded and
sliced
300 ml/½ pint chicken stock
2 tbsp freshly chopped
coriander
freshly cooked noodles, to
serve

1 Using a sharp knife, trim the pork, discarding any sinew or fat. Cut into 2 cm/¾ inch slices and place in a shallow dish. Blend the soy sauce and cornflour together until smooth and free from lumps, then pour over the pork. Stir until coated in the cornflour mixture, then cover with clingfilm and leave to marinate in the refrigerator for at least 30 minutes.

2 Heat a nonstick frying pan until hot, add the cashew nuts and dry-fry for 2–3 minutes, or until toasted, stirring frequently. Transfer to a plate and reserve.

3 Heat a wok or large frying pan, add 2 tablespoons of the oil and when hot, add the leeks, ginger, garlic and pepper and stir-fry for 5 minutes or until softened. Using a slotted spoon, transfer to a plate and keep warm.

4 Drain the pork, reserving the marinade. Add the remaining oil to the wok and when hot, add the pork and stir-fry for 5 minutes or until browned. Return the reserved vegetables to the wok with the marinade and the stock. Bring to the boil, then simmer for 2 minutes, or until the sauce has thickened. Stir in the toasted cashew nuts and chopped coriander and serve immediately with freshly cooked noodles.

FOOD FACT

Now grown throughout the tropics, cashew nuts originated in South America. The fruit is large, shiny and pink, red or yellow in colour and is sometimes made into a drink or jam. The small hard-shelled kidney-shaped seed in the centre of the fruit contains the cashew nut.

LAMB MEATBALLS WITH SAVOY CABBAGE

INGREDIENTS   Serves 4

450 g/1 lb fresh lamb mince
1 tbsp freshly chopped parsley
1 tbsp freshly grated root
  ginger
1 tbsp light soy sauce
1 medium egg yolk
4 tbsp dark soy sauce
2 tbsp dry sherry
1 tbsp cornflour
3 tbsp vegetable oil

2 garlic cloves, peeled and
  chopped
1 bunch spring onions,
  trimmed and shredded
½ Savoy cabbage, trimmed
  and shredded
½ head Chinese leaves,
  trimmed and shredded
freshly chopped red chilli, to
  garnish

1 Place the lamb mince in a large bowl with the parsley, ginger, light soy sauce and egg yolk and mix together. Divide the mixture into walnut-sized pieces and using your hands roll into balls. Place on a baking sheet, cover with clingfilm and chill in the refrigerator for at least 30 minutes.

2 Meanwhile, blend together the dark soy sauce, sherry and cornflour with 2 tablespoons of water in a small bowl until smooth. Reserve.

3 Heat a wok, add the oil and when hot, add the meatballs and cook for 5–8 minutes, or until browned all over, turning occasionally. Using a slotted spoon, transfer the meatballs to a large plate and keep warm.

4 Add the garlic, spring onions, Savoy cabbage and the Chinese leaves to the wok and stir-fry for 3 minutes. Pour over the reserved soy sauce mixture, bring to the boil, then simmer for 30 seconds or until thickened. Return the meatballs to the wok and mix in. Garnish with chopped red chilli and serve immediately.

TASTY TIP

This dish is made with simple, basic ingredients, but you can substitute more Chinese ingredients if you prefer, such as rice wine vinegar instead of sherry and pak choi leaves instead of Savoy cabbage. As the meatballs contain raw egg, make sure that they are cooked thoroughly.

BARBECUED PORK FILLET

INGREDIENTS

Serves 4

2 tbsp clear honey

2 tbsp hoisin sauce

2 tsp tomato purée

2.5 cm/1 inch piece fresh root ginger, peeled and chopped

450 g/1 lb pork tenderloin

3 tbsp vegetable oil

1 garlic clove, peeled and chopped

1 bunch spring onions, trimmed and chopped

1 red pepper, deseeded and cut into chunks

1 yellow pepper, deseeded and cut into chunks

350 g/12 oz cooked long-grain rice

125 g/4 oz frozen peas, thawed

2 tbsp light soy sauce

1 tbsp sesame oil

50 g/2 oz toasted flaked almonds

1 Preheat the oven to 200°C/400°F/Gas Mark 6, 15 minutes before cooking. Mix together the honey, hoisin sauce, tomato purée and ginger in a bowl. Trim the pork, discarding any sinew or fat. Place in a shallow dish and spread the honey and hoisin sauce over the pork to cover completely. Cover with clingfilm and chill in the refrigerator for 4 hours, turning occasionally.

2 Remove the pork from the marinade and place in a roasting tin, reserving the marinade. Cook in the preheated oven for 20–25 minutes, or until the pork is tender and the juices run clear when pierced with a skewer. Baste occasionally during cooking with the reserved marinade. Remove the pork from the oven, leave to rest for 5 minutes, then slice thinly and keep warm.

3 Meanwhile, heat a wok or large frying pan, add the vegetable oil and when hot, add the garlic, spring onions and peppers and stir-fry for 4 minutes or until softened. Add the rice and peas and stir-fry for 2 minutes.

4 Add the soy sauce, sesame oil and flaked almonds and stir-fry for 30 seconds or until heated through. Tip into a warmed serving dish and top with the sliced pork. Serve immediately.

HELPFUL HINT

If you have only untoasted flaked almonds, place them on a baking sheet in the oven for 5–10 minutes while you cook the pork. Check them frequently as nuts burn very easily.

SPICY LAMB & PEPPERS

INGREDIENTS   Serves 4

550 g/1¼ lb lamb fillet
4 tbsp soy sauce
1 tbsp dry sherry
1 tbsp cornflour
3 tbsp vegetable oil
1 bunch spring onions,
  shredded
225 g/8 oz broccoli florets
2 garlic cloves, peeled and
  chopped
2.5 cm/1 inch piece fresh root
  ginger, peeled and cut into
  matchsticks

1 red pepper, deseeded and
  cut into chunks
1 green pepper, deseeded and
  cut into chunks
2 tsp Chinese five spice
  powder
1–2 tsp dried crushed chillies,
  or to taste
1 tbsp tomato purée
1 tbsp rice wine vinegar
1 tbsp soft brown sugar
freshly cooked noodles, to
  serve

1 Cut the lamb into 2 cm/¾ inch slices, then place in a shallow dish. Blend the soy sauce, sherry and cornflour together in a small bowl and pour over the lamb. Turn the lamb until coated lightly with the marinade. Cover with clingfilm and leave to marinate in the refrigerator for at least 30 minutes, turning occasionally.

2 Heat a wok or large frying pan, add the oil and when hot, stir-fry the spring onions and broccoli for 2 minutes. Add the garlic, ginger and peppers and stir-fry for a further 2 minutes. Using a slotted spoon, transfer the vegetables to a plate and keep warm.

3 Using a slotted spoon, lift the lamb from the marinade, shaking off any excess marinade. Add to the wok and stir-fry for 5 minutes, or until browned all over. Reserve the marinade.

4 Return the vegetables to the wok and stir in the Chinese five spice powder, chillies, tomato purée, reserved marinade, vinegar and sugar. Bring to the boil, stirring constantly, until thickened. Simmer for 2 minutes or until heated through thoroughly. Serve immediately with noodles.

FOOD FACT

Chinese rice wine, or *Shaoxing*, is used for both drinking and cooking and is an essential ingredient in banquet dishes. If it is unavailable, dry sherry may be substituted.

BRANDIED LAMB CHOPS

INGREDIENTS   Serves 4

8 lamb loin chops
3 tbsp groundnut oil
5 cm/2 inch piece fresh root
  ginger, peeled and cut into
  matchsticks
2 garlic cloves, peeled and
  chopped
225 g/8 oz button mushrooms,
  wiped and halved if large
2 tbsp light soy sauce
2 tbsp dry sherry

1 tbsp brandy
1 tsp Chinese five spice
  powder
1 tsp soft brown sugar
200 ml/7 fl oz lamb or chicken
  stock
1 tsp sesame oil

TO SERVE:
freshly cooked rice
freshly stir-fried vegetables

1 Using a sharp knife, trim the lamb chops, discarding any sinew or fat. Heat a wok or large frying pan, add the oil and when hot, add the lamb chops and cook for 3 minutes on each side or until browned. Using a fish slice, transfer the lamb chops to a plate and keep warm.

2 Add the ginger, garlic and button mushrooms to the wok and stir-fry for 3 minutes or until the mushrooms have browned.

3 Return the lamb chops to the wok together with the soy sauce, sherry, brandy, five spice powder and sugar. Pour in the stock, bring to the boil, then reduce the heat slightly and simmer for 4–5 minutes, or until the lamb is tender, ensuring that the liquid does not evaporate completely. Add the sesame oil and heat for a further 30 seconds.

Turn into a warmed serving dish and serve immediately with freshly cooked rice and stir-fried vegetables.

FOOD FACT

Lamb is not widely eaten in China, but Chinese Muslims (who are forbidden to eat pork) often cook it as do Mongols and people from Sinkiang. Use a good-quality stock for this dish, preferably one without too much salt as the sauce is reduced slightly. Choose either a home-made one or a supermarket tub of fresh stock.

DUCK IN BLACK BEAN SAUCE

INGREDIENTS   Serves 4

450 g/1 lb duck breast, skinned
1 tbsp light soy sauce
1 tbsp Chinese rice wine or
  dry sherry
2.5 cm/1 inch piece fresh root
  ginger
3 garlic cloves
2 spring onions

2 tbsp Chinese preserved
  black beans
1 tbsp groundnut or vegetable
  oil
150 ml/¼ pint chicken stock
shredded spring onions, to
  garnish
freshly cooked noodles, to serve

1 Using a sharp knife, trim the duck breasts, removing any fat. Slice thickly and place in a shallow dish. Mix together the soy sauce and Chinese rice wine or sherry and pour over the duck. Leave to marinate for 1 hour in the refrigerator, then drain and discard the marinade.

2 Peel the ginger and chop finely. Peel the garlic cloves and either chop finely or crush. Trim the root from the spring onions, discard the outer leaves and chop. Finely chop the black beans.

3 Heat a wok or large frying pan, add the oil and when very hot, add the ginger, garlic, spring onions and black beans and stir-fry for 30 seconds. Add the drained duck and stir-fry for 3–5 minutes or until the duck is browned.

4 Add the chicken stock to the wok, bring to the boil, then reduce the heat and simmer for 5 minutes, or until the duck is cooked and the sauce is reduced and thickened. Remove from the heat. Tip on to a bed of freshly cooked noodles, garnish with spring onion shreds and serve immediately.

HELPFUL HINT

The way in which a dish is presented and garnished is extremely important in both Chinese and Thai cuisine. Fine shreds of colourful vegetables are simple to make. For spring onion shreds, cut off most of the white bulb end and trim the tops. Cut the remaining green part lengthways into fine shreds. These can be curled by dropping them into iced water for a few minutes.

CHINESE-GLAZED POUSSIN WITH GREEN & BLACK RICE

INGREDIENTS

Serves 4

4 oven-ready poussins
salt and freshly ground black
  pepper
300 ml/½ pint apple juice
1 cinnamon stick
2 star anise
½ tsp Chinese five spice
  powder
50 g/2 oz dark muscovado
  sugar
2 tbsp tomato ketchup

1 tbsp cider vinegar
grated rind of 1 orange
350 g/12 oz mixed basmati
  white and wild rice
125 g/4 oz mangetout, finely
  sliced lengthways
1 bunch spring onions,
  trimmed and finely shredded
  lengthways
salt and freshly ground black
  pepper

1 Preheat the oven to 200°C/ 400°F/Gas Mark 6, 15 minutes before cooking. Rinse the poussins inside and out and pat dry with absorbent kitchen paper. Using tweezers, remove any feathers. Season well with salt and pepper, then reserve.

2 Pour the apple juice into a small saucepan and add the cinnamon stick, star anise and Chinese five spice powder. Bring to the boil, then simmer rapidly until reduced by half. Reduce the heat, stir in the sugar, tomato ketchup, vinegar and orange rind and simmer gently until the sugar is dissolved and the glaze is syrupy. Remove from the heat and leave to cool completely. Remove the whole spices.

3 Place the poussins on a wire rack set over a tinfoil-lined roasting tin. Brush generously with the apple glaze. Roast in the preheated oven for 40–45 minutes, or until the juices run clear when the thigh is pierced with a skewer, basting once or twice with the remaining glaze. Remove the poussins from the oven and leave to cool slightly.

4 Meanwhile, cook the rice according to the packet instructions. Bring a large saucepan of lightly salted water to the boil and add the mangetout. Blanch for 1 minute, then drain thoroughly. As soon as the rice is cooked, drain and transfer to a warmed bowl. Add the mangetout and spring onions, season to taste and stir well. Arrange on warmed dinner plates, place a poussin on top and serve immediately.

BRAISED CHICKEN WITH AUBERGINE

INGREDIENTS
Serves 4

3 tbsp vegetable oil
12 chicken thighs
2 large aubergines, trimmed and cubed
4 garlic cloves, peeled and crushed
2 tsp freshly grated root ginger
900 ml/1½ pints vegetable stock
2 tbsp light soy sauce

2 tbsp Chinese preserved black beans
6 spring onions, trimmed and thinly sliced diagonally
1 tbsp cornflour
1 tbsp sesame oil
spring onion tassels, to garnish
freshly cooked noodles or rice, to serve

1 Heat a wok or large frying pan, add the oil and when hot, add the chicken thighs and cook over a medium high heat for 5 minutes, or until browned all over. Transfer to a large plate and keep warm.

2 Add the aubergine to the wok and cook over a high heat for 5 minutes or until browned, turning occasionally. Add the garlic and ginger and stir-fry for 1 minute.

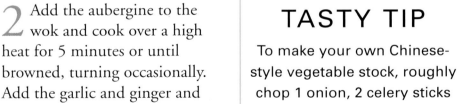

3 Return the chicken to the wok, pour in the stock and add the soy sauce and black beans. Bring to the boil, then simmer for 20 minutes, or until the chicken is tender. Add the spring onions after 10 minutes.

4 Blend the cornflour with 2 tablespoons of water. Stir into the wok and simmer until the sauce has thickened. Stir in the sesame oil, heat for 30 seconds, then remove from the heat. Garnish with spring onion tassels and serve immediately with noodles or rice.

TASTY TIP

To make your own Chinese-style vegetable stock, roughly chop 1 onion, 2 celery sticks and 2 carrots and place in a large saucepan with a few dried shiitake mushrooms and slices of fresh root ginger. Pour in 1.4 litres/2½ pints cold water, bring to the boil, partially cover and simmer for 30 minutes. Leave to cool, then strain through a fine sieve, discarding the vegetables. Store in the refrigerator.

STIR-FRIED DUCK WITH CASHEWS

INGREDIENTS   Serves 4

450 g/1 lb duck breast, skinned
3 tbsp groundnut oil
1 garlic clove, peeled and
   finely chopped
1 tsp freshly grated ginger root
1 carrot, peeled and sliced
125 g/4 oz mangetout, trimmed
2 tsp Chinese rice wine or dry
   sherry

1 tbsp light soy sauce
1 tsp cornflour
50 g/2 oz unsalted cashew
   nuts, roasted
1 spring onion, trimmed and
   finely chopped
1 spring onion, shredded
boiled or steamed rice, to serve

1 Trim the duck breasts, discarding any fat and slice thickly. Heat the wok, add 2 tablespoons of the oil and when hot, add the sliced duck breast. Cook for 3–4 minutes or until sealed. Using a slotted spoon, remove from the wok and leave to drain on absorbent kitchen paper.

2 Wipe the wok clean and return to the heat. Add the remaining oil and when hot, add the garlic and ginger. Stir-fry for 30 seconds, then add the carrot and mangetout. Stir-fry for a further 2 minutes, then pour in the Chinese rice wine or sherry and soy sauce.

3 Blend the cornflour with 1 teaspoon of water and stir into the wok. Mix well and bring to the boil. Return the duck slices to the wok and simmer for 5 minutes, or until the meat and vegetables are tender. Add the cashews, then remove the wok from the heat.

4 Sprinkle over the chopped and shredded spring onion and serve immediately with plain boiled or steamed rice.

HELPFUL HINT

Mangetout are now available all-year round. Look for small bright green mangetout containing flat, barely formed peas and not large bumps. Store them in the refrigerator for no more than 2 days before using, to maximise their fresh sweet flavour. To prepare, simply top and tail, pulling away as much string from the edges as you can. Dry-fry the cashew nuts in the wok before starting to seal the duck breasts. Ensure the nuts do not burn.

STIR-FRIED LEMON CHICKEN

INGREDIENTS Serves 4

350 g/12 oz boneless, skinless chicken breast
1 large egg white
5 tsp cornflour
3 tbsp vegetable or groundnut oil
150 ml/¼ pint chicken stock
2 tbsp fresh lemon juice
2 tbsp light soy sauce
1 tbsp Chinese rice wine or dry sherry

1 tbsp sugar
2 garlic cloves, peeled and finely chopped
¼ tsp dried chilli flakes, or to taste

TO GARNISH:
lemon rind strips
red chilli slices

1 Using a sharp knife, trim the chicken, discarding any fat and cut into thin strips, about 5 cm/2 inch long and 1 cm/½ inch wide. Place in a shallow dish. Lightly whisk the egg white and 1 tablespoon of the cornflour together until smooth. Pour over the chicken strips and mix well until coated evenly. Leave to marinate in the refrigerator for at least 20 minutes.

2 When ready to cook, drain the chicken and reserve. Heat a wok or large frying pan, add the oil and when hot, add the chicken and stir-fry for 1–2 minutes, or until the chicken has turned white. Using a slotted spoon, remove from the wok and reserve.

3 Wipe the wok clean and return to the heat. Add the chicken stock, lemon juice, soy sauce, Chinese rice wine or sherry,

sugar, garlic and chilli flakes and bring to the boil. Blend the remaining cornflour with 1 tablespoon of water and stir into the stock. Simmer for 1 minute.

4 Return the chicken to the wok and continue simmering for a further 2–3 minutes, or until the chicken is tender and the sauce has thickened. Garnish with lemon strips and red chilli slices. Serve immediately.

FOOD FACT

Chilli flakes are crushed dried red chillies and are widely used in parts of China where long strings of red chillies can be seen drying in the sun.

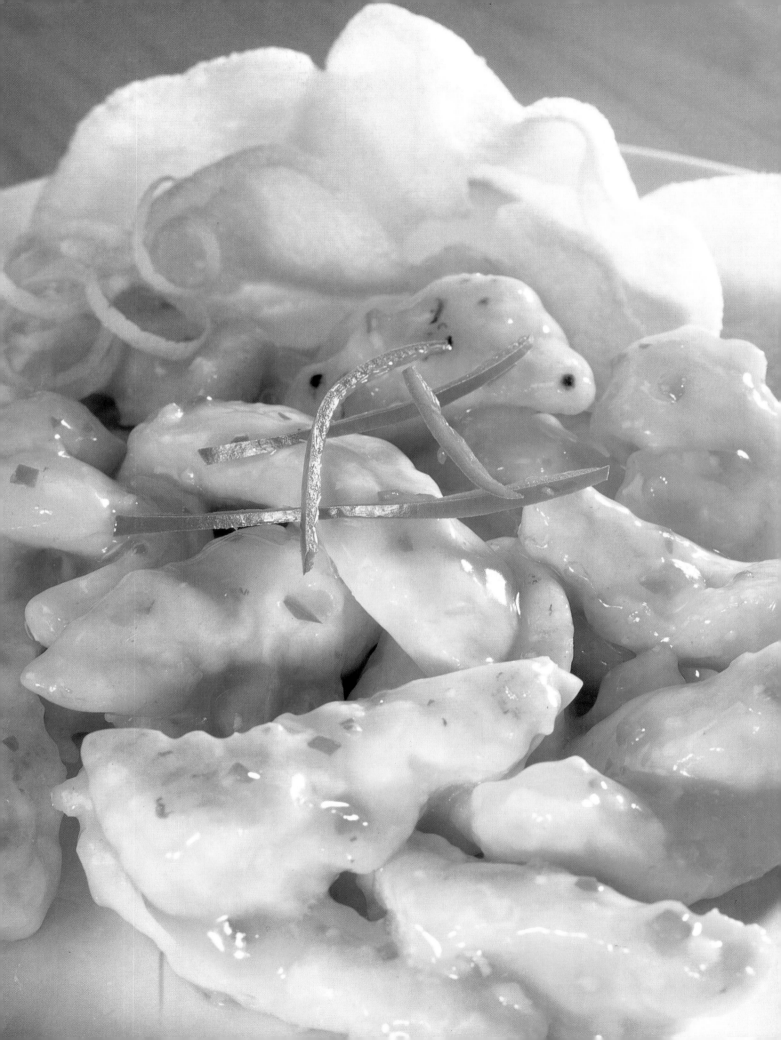

TURKEY & VEGETABLE STIR FRY

INGREDIENTS — Serves 4

350 g/12 oz mixed vegetables, such as baby sweetcorn, 1 small red pepper, pak choi, mushrooms, broccoli florets and baby carrots
1 red chilli
2 tbsp groundnut oil
350 g/12 oz skinless, boneless turkey breast, sliced into fine strips across the grain
2 garlic cloves, peeled and finely chopped
2.5 cm/1 inch piece fresh root ginger, peeled and finely grated

3 spring onions, trimmed and finely sliced
2 tbsp light soy sauce
1 tbsp Chinese rice wine or dry sherry
2 tbsp chicken stock or water
1 tsp cornflour
1 tsp sesame oil
freshly cooked noodles or rice, to serve

TO GARNISH:
50 g/2 oz toasted cashew nuts
2 spring onions, finely shredded
25 g/1 oz beansprouts

1 Slice or chop the vegetables into small pieces, depending on which you use. Halve the baby sweetcorn lengthways, deseed and thinly slice the red pepper, tear or shred the pak choi, slice the mushrooms, break the broccoli into small florets and cut the carrots into matchsticks. Deseed and finely chop the chilli.

2 Heat a wok or large frying pan, add the oil and when hot, add the turkey strips and stir-fry for 1 minute or until they turn white. Add the garlic, ginger, spring onions and chilli and cook for a few seconds.

3 Add the prepared carrot, pepper, broccoli and mushrooms and stir-fry for 1 minute. Add the baby sweetcorn and pak choi and stir-fry for 1 minute.

4 Blend the soy sauce, Chinese rice wine or sherry and stock or water and pour over the vegetables. Blend the cornflour with 1 teaspoon of water and stir into the vegetables, mixing well. Bring to the boil, reduce the heat, then simmer for 1 minute. Stir in the sesame oil. Tip into a warmed serving dish, sprinkle with cashew nuts, shredded spring onions and beansprouts. Serve immediately with noodles or rice.

FOOD FACT

Beansprouts come from the mung bean.

CRISPY ROAST DUCK LEGS WITH PANCAKES

INGREDIENTS
Serves 6

900 g/2 lb plums, halved
25 g/1 oz butter
2 star anise
1 tsp freshly grated root
  ginger
50 g/2 oz soft brown sugar
zest and juice of 1 orange
salt and freshly ground black
  pepper

4 duck legs
3 tbsp dark soy sauce
2 tbsp dark brown sugar
½ cucumber, cut into
  matchsticks
1 small bunch spring onions,
  trimmed and shredded
18 ready-made Chinese
  pancakes, warmed

1 Preheat the oven to 220°C/ 425°F/Gas Mark 7, 15 minutes before cooking. Discard stones from plums and place in a saucepan with the butter, star anise, ginger, brown sugar and orange zest and juice. Season to taste with pepper. Cook over a gentle heat until the sugar has dissolved. Bring to the boil, then reduce heat and simmer for 15 minutes, stirring occasionally until the plums are soft and the mixture is thick. Remove the star anise. Leave to cool.

2 Using a fork, prick the duck legs all over. Place in a large bowl and pour boiling water over to remove some of the fat. Drain, pat dry on absorbent kitchen paper and leave until cold.

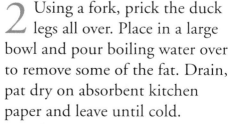

3 Mix together the soy sauce, dark brown sugar and the ½ teaspoon of salt. Rub this mixture generously over the duck legs.

Transfer to a wire rack set over a roasting tin and roast in the preheated oven for 30–40 minutes, or until well cooked and the skin is browned and crisp. Remove from the oven and leave to rest for 10 minutes.

4 Shred the duck meat using a fork to hold the hot duck leg and another to remove the meat. Transfer to a warmed serving platter with the cucumber and spring onions. Serve immediately with the plum compote and warmed pancakes.

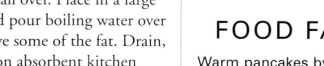

FOOD FACT

Warm pancakes by stacking and wrapping in tinfoil and placing on a plate in a steamer or for 15 minutes in the oven, after removing the duck and turning the oven off.

CHINESE BARBECUE-STYLE QUAILS WITH AUBERGINES

INGREDIENTS   Serves 6

4 quails

2 tbsp salt

3 tbsp hoisin sauce

1 tbsp Chinese rice wine or
   dry sherry

1 tbsp light soy sauce

700 g/1½ lb aubergines,
   trimmed and cubed

1 tbsp oil

4 garlic cloves, peeled and
   finely chopped

1 tbsp freshly chopped root
   ginger

6 spring onions, trimmed and
   finely chopped

3 tbsp dark soy sauce

¼ tsp dried chilli flakes

1 tbsp yellow bean sauce

1 tbsp sugar

TO GARNISH:

sprigs of fresh coriander

sliced red chilli

1 Preheat the oven to 240°C/ 475°F/Gas Mark 9. Rub the quails inside and out with 1 tablespoon of the salt. Mix together the hoisin sauce, Chinese rice wine or sherry and light soy sauce. Rub the quails inside and out with the sauce. Transfer to a small roasting tin and roast in the preheated oven for 5 minutes. Reduce the heat to 180°C/350°F/Gas Mark 4 and continue to roast for 20 minutes. Turn the oven off and leave the quails for 5 minutes, then remove and leave to rest for 10 minutes.

2 Place the aubergine in a colander and sprinkle with the remaining salt. Leave to drain for 20 minutes, then rinse under cold running water and pat dry with absorbent kitchen paper.

3 Heat a wok or large frying pan over a moderate heat. Add the oil and when hot, add the aubergines, garlic, ginger and 4 of the spring onions and cook for 1 minute. Add the dark soy sauce, chilli flakes, yellow bean sauce, sugar and 450 ml/¾ pint of water. Bring to the boil, then simmer uncovered for 10–15 minutes.

4 Increase the heat to high and continue to cook, stirring occasionally, until the sauce is reduced and slightly thickened. Spoon the aubergine mixture on to warmed individual plates and top with a quail. Garnish with the remaining spring onion, fresh chilli and a sprig of coriander and serve immediately.

CHINESE BRAISED WHITE CHICKEN WITH THREE SAUCES

INGREDIENTS   Serves 4

1.4 kg/3 lb oven-ready chicken
salt
6 spring onions, trimmed
5 cm/2 inch piece fresh root
    ginger, peeled and sliced
2 tsp Szechuan peppercorns,
    crushed
2½ tsp sea salt flakes or
    crushed coarse sea salt
2 tsp freshly grated root ginger
4 tbsp dark soy sauce
4 tbsp sunflower oil

1 tsp caster sugar
2 garlic cloves, finely chopped
3 tbsp light soy sauce
1 tbsp Chinese rice wine or
    dry sherry
1 tsp sesame oil
3 tbsp rice vinegar
1 small hot red chilli,
    deseeded and finely sliced
spring onion curls, to garnish
freshly steamed saffron-
    flavoured rice, to serve

1 Remove any fat from inside the chicken, rub inside and out with ½ teaspoon of salt and leave for 20 minutes. Place 3.4 litres/6 pints water with 2 spring onions and the ginger in a saucepan and bring to the boil. Add the chicken, breast-side down, return to the boil, cover and simmer for 20 minutes. Remove from the heat and leave for 1 hour. Remove the chicken and leave to cool.

2 Dry-fry the Szechuan peppercorns in a nonstick frying pan until they darken slightly and smell aromatic. Crush, mix with the sea salt and reserve.

3 Squeeze the juice from half of the grated ginger, mix with the dark soy sauce, 1 tablespoon of the sunflower oil and half the sugar. Reserve.

4 Finely chop the remaining spring onions and mix with the remaining ginger and garlic in a bowl. Heat the remaining oil to smoking and pour over the onion and ginger. When they stop sizzling, stir in the light soy sauce, Chinese rice wine or sherry and sesame oil. Reserve.

5 Mix together the rice vinegar, remaining sugar and chilli. Stir until the sugar dissolves. Reserve.

6 Remove the skin from the chicken, then remove the legs and cut them in 2 at the joint. Lift the breast meat away from the carcass in 2 pieces and slice thickly crossways. Sprinkle the pepper and salt mixture over the chicken, garnish with spring onion curls and serve with the dipping sauces, spring onion mixture and rice.

ORANGE ROASTED WHOLE CHICKEN

INGREDIENTS   Serves 6

1 small orange, thinly sliced
50 g/2 oz sugar
1.4 kg/3 lb oven-ready chicken
1 small bunch fresh coriander
1 small bunch fresh mint
2 tbsp olive oil
1 tsp Chinese five spice powder
½ tsp paprika

1 tsp fennel seeds, crushed
salt and freshly ground black
  pepper
sprigs of fresh coriander,
  to garnish
freshly cooked vegetables,
  to serve

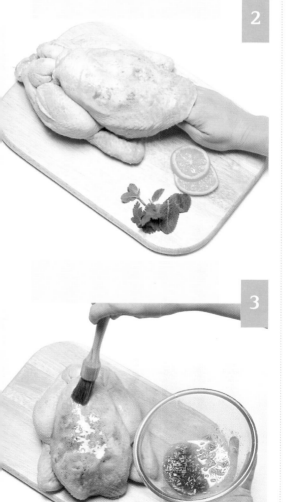

1 Preheat the oven to 190°C/ 375°F/Gas Mark 5, 10 minutes before cooking. Place the orange slices in a small saucepan, cover with water, bring to the boil, then simmer for 2 minutes and drain. Place the sugar in a clean saucepan with 150 ml/¼ pint fresh water. Stir over a low heat until the sugar dissolves, then bring to the boil, add the drained orange slices and simmer for 10 minutes. Remove from the heat and leave in the syrup until cold.

2 Remove any excess fat from inside the chicken. Starting at the neck end, carefully loosen the skin of the chicken over the breast and legs without tearing. Push the orange slices under the loosened skin with the coriander and mint.

3 Mix together the olive oil, Chinese five spice powder, paprika and crushed fennel seeds and season to taste with salt and pepper. Brush the chicken skin

generously with this mixture. Transfer to a wire rack set over a roasting tin and roast in the preheated oven for 1½ hours, or until the juices run clear when a skewer is inserted into the thickest part of the thigh. Remove from the oven and leave to rest for 10 minutes. Garnish with sprigs of fresh coriander and serve with freshly cooked vegetables.

TASTY TIP

To make oven-baked rice, soften a chopped onion in 1 tablespoon sunflower oil in an ovenproof casserole. Stir in 250 g/9 oz long-grain rice, then remove from the heat. Pour in 750 ml/1¼ pints chicken or vegetable stock, 1 star anise, ½ cinnamon stick, 1 bay leaf, salt and pepper. Cover and cook for 45 minutes or until tender. Fluff up with a fork and remove the spices.

BAKED THAI CHICKEN WINGS

INGREDIENTS   Serves 4

4 tbsp clear honey
1 tbsp chilli sauce
1 garlic clove, peeled and
   crushed
1 tsp freshly grated root ginger
1 lemon grass stalk, outer
   leaves discarded and finely
   chopped
2 tbsp lime zest
3–4 tbsp freshly squeezed lime
   juice

1 tbsp light soy sauce
1 tsp ground cumin
1 tsp ground coriander
¼ tsp ground cinnamon
1.4 kg/3 lb chicken wings
   (about 12 large wings)
6 tbsp mayonnaise
2 tbsp freshly chopped
   coriander
lemon or lime wedges, to
   garnish

1 Preheat the oven to 190°C/
375°F/Gas Mark 5, 10
minutes before cooking. In a
small saucepan, mix together the
honey, chilli sauce, garlic, ginger,
lemon grass, 1 tablespoon of the
lime zest and 2 tablespoons of the
lime juice with the soy sauce,
cumin, coriander and cinnamon.
Heat gently until just starting to
bubble, then remove from the
heat and leave to cool.

2 Prepare the chicken wings by
folding the tips back under
the thickest part of the meat to
form a triangle. Arrange in a
shallow ovenproof dish. Pour
over the honey mixture, turning
the wings to ensure that they
are all well coated. Cover with
clingfilm and leave to marinate
in the refrigerator for 4 hours or
overnight, turning once or twice.

3 Mix together the mayonnaise
with the remaining lime zest

and juice and the coriander.
Leave to let the flavours develop
while the wings are cooking.

4 Arrange the wings on a
rack set over a tinfoil-lined
roasting tin. Roast at the top of
the preheated oven for 50–60
minutes, or until the wings are
tender and golden, basting once or
twice with the remaining marinade
and turning once. Remove from
the oven. Garnish the wings with
lemon or lime wedges and serve
immediately with the mayonnaise.

HELPFUL HINT

Alternatively, you could serve a
spicy dipping sauce by mixing
together 1 tablespoon lime zest
and juice with 2 small fresh red
Thai chillies, deseeded and
sliced, 1 tablespoon caster
sugar, 3 tablespoons fish sauce
and 1 tablespoon water.

GRILLED SPICED CHICKEN WITH TOMATO & SHALLOT CHUTNEY

INGREDIENTS   Serves 4

3 tbsp sunflower oil

2 hot red chillies, deseeded and chopped

3 garlic cloves, peeled and chopped

1 tsp ground turmeric

1 tsp cumin seeds

1 tsp fennel seeds

1 tbsp freshly chopped basil

1 tbsp dark brown sugar

125 ml/4 fl oz rice or white wine vinegar

2 tsp sesame oil

4 large chicken breast quarters, wings attached

225 g/8 oz small shallots, peeled and halved

2 tbsp Chinese rice wine or dry sherry

50 g/2 oz caster sugar

175 g/6 oz cherry tomatoes, halved

2 tbsp light soy sauce

TO GARNISH:

sprigs of fresh coriander

sprigs of fresh dill

lemon wedges

1 Preheat the grill to medium, 5 minutes before cooking. Heat a wok or large frying pan, add 1 tablespoon of the sunflower oil and when hot, add the chillies, garlic, turmeric, cumin, fennel seeds, and basil. Fry for 5 minutes, add the sugar and 2 tablespoons of vinegar and stir until the sugar has dissolved. Remove, stir in the sesame oil and leave to cool.

2 Cut 3 or 4 deep slashes in the thickest part of the chicken breasts. Spread the spice paste over the chicken, place in a dish, cover and marinate in the refrigerator for at least 4 hours or overnight.

3 Heat the remaining sunflower oil in a saucepan, add the shallots and remaining garlic and cook gently for 15 minutes. Add the remaining vinegar, Chinese rice wine or sherry and caster sugar with 50 ml/2 fl oz water. Bring to the boil and simmer rapidly for 10 minutes, or until thickened. Add the tomatoes with the soy sauce. Simmer for 5–10 minutes, or until the liquid is reduced. Leave the chutney to cool.

4 Transfer the chicken pieces to a grill pan and cook under the preheated grill for 15–20 minutes on each side, or until the chicken is cooked through, basting frequently. Garnish with coriander sprigs and lemon wedges and serve immediately with the chutney.

SEARED DUCK WITH PICKLED PLUMS

INGREDIENTS

Serves 4

4 small skinless, boneless
  duck breasts
2 garlic cloves, peeled and
  crushed
1 tsp hot chilli sauce
2 tsp clear honey
2 tsp dark brown sugar
juice of 1 lime
1 tbsp dark soy sauce
6 large plums, halved and
  stones removed

50 g/2 oz caster sugar
50 ml/2 fl oz white wine vinegar
¼ tsp dried chilli flakes
¼ tsp ground cinnamon
1 tbsp sunflower oil
150 ml/¼ pint chicken stock
2 tbsp oyster sauce
sprigs of fresh flat leaf parsley,
  to garnish
freshly cooked noodles, to
  serve

1 Cut a few deep slashes in each duck breast and place in a shallow dish. Mix together the garlic, chilli sauce, honey, brown sugar, lime juice and soy sauce. Spread over the duck and leave to marinate in the refrigerator for 4 hours or overnight, if time permits, turning occasionally.

2 Place the plums in a saucepan with the caster sugar, white wine vinegar, chilli flakes and cinnamon and bring to the boil. Simmer gently for 5 minutes, or until the plums have just softened, then leave to cool.

3 Remove the duck from the marinade and pat dry with absorbent kitchen paper. Reserve the marinade. Heat a wok or large frying pan, add the oil and when hot, brown the duck on both sides. Pour in the stock,

oyster sauce and reserved marinade and simmer for 5 minutes. Remove the duck and keep warm.

4 Remove the plums from their liquid and reserve. Pour the liquid into the duck sauce, bring to the boil, then simmer, uncovered, for 5 minutes, or until reduced and thickened. Arrange the duck on warmed plates. Divide the plums between the plates and spoon over the sauce. Garnish with parsley and serve immediately with noodles.

HELPFUL HINT

When marinating use a glass or glazed earthenware dish. Plastic dishes will absorb the smell and colour of marinades; metal may react with acidic ingredients.

THAI STUFFED OMELETTE

INGREDIENTS   Serves 4

1 shallot, peeled and roughly chopped

1 garlic clove, peeled and roughly chopped

1 small red chilli, deseeded and roughly chopped

15 g/½ oz coriander leaves

pinch of sugar

2 tsp light soy sauce

2 tsp Thai fish sauce

4 tbsp vegetable or groundnut oil

175 g/6 oz skinless, boneless chicken breast, finely sliced

½ small aubergine, trimmed and diced

50 g/2 oz button or shiitake mushrooms, wiped and sliced

½ small red pepper, deseeded and sliced

50 g/2 oz fine green beans, trimmed and halved

2 spring onions, trimmed and thickly sliced

25 g/1 oz peas, thawed if frozen

6 medium eggs

salt and freshly ground black pepper

sprig of fresh basil, to garnish

1 Place the shallot, garlic, chilli, coriander and sugar in the bowl of a spice grinder or food processor. Blend until finely chopped. Add the soy sauce, fish sauce and 1 tablespoon of the vegetable oil and blend briefly to mix into a paste. Reserve.

2 Heat a wok or large frying pan, add 1 tablespoon of the oil and when hot, add the chicken and aubergine and stir-fry for 3–4 minutes, or until golden. Add the mushrooms, red pepper, green beans and spring onions and stir-fry for 3–4 minutes or until tender, adding the peas for the final 1 minute. Remove from the heat and stir in the reserved coriander paste. Reserve.

3 Beat the eggs in a bowl and season to taste with salt and pepper. Heat the remaining oil in a large nonstick frying pan and add the eggs, tilting the pan so that the eggs cover the bottom. Stir the eggs until they are starting to set all over, then cook for 1–2 minutes, or until firm and set on the bottom but still slightly soft on top.

4 Spoon the chicken and vegetable mixture on to one-half of the omelette and carefully flip the other half over. Cook over a low heat for 2–3 minutes, or until the omelette is set and the chicken and vegetables are heated through. Garnish with a sprig of basil and serve immediately.

RED CHICKEN CURRY

INGREDIENTS   Serves 4

225 ml/8 fl oz coconut cream
2 tbsp vegetable oil
2 garlic clove, peeled and
   finely chopped
2 tbsp Thai red curry paste
2 tbsp Thai fish sauce
2 tsp sugar

350 g/12 oz boneless, skinless
   chicken breast, finely sliced
450 ml/¾ pint chicken stock
2 lime leaves, shredded
chopped red chilli, to garnish
freshly boiled rice or steamed
   Thai fragrant rice, to serve

1 Pour the coconut cream into a small saucepan and heat gently. Meanwhile, heat a wok or large frying pan and add the oil. When the oil is very hot, swirl the oil around the wok until the wok is lightly coated, then add the garlic and stir-fry for about 10–20 seconds, or until the garlic begins to brown. Add the curry paste and stir-fry for a few more seconds, then pour in the warmed coconut cream.

2 Cook the coconut cream mixture for 5 minutes, or until the cream has curdled and thickened. Stir in the fish sauce and sugar. Add the finely sliced chicken breast and cook for 3–4 minutes, or until the chicken has turned white.

3 Pour the stock into the wok, bring to the boil, then simmer for 1–2 minutes, or until the chicken is cooked through. Stir in the shredded lime leaves. Turn into a warmed serving dish, garnish with chopped red chilli and serve immediately with rice.

TASTY TIP

Thai fragrant rice has a soft, light fluffy texture. In Thailand it is usually cooked by the following method, starting with cold rather than boiling water to retain its delicate flavour. For 4 people, put enough rice to come up to the 400 ml (14 fl oz) level of a measuring jug. Rinse under cold running water then place in a heavy-based saucepan with 600 ml/1 pint cold water – the water should come 2.5 cm/1 inch above the rice. Add a large pinch of salt, bring to the boil, then simmer for 15 minutes, or until most of the water has evaporated. Cover with a tight-fitting lid, turn the heat to as low as possible and cook for a further 5 minutes, or until all the water has been absorbed and the rice is tender. For added flavour, a light stock can be used instead of the water.

GREEN TURKEY CURRY

INGREDIENTS   Serves 4

4 baby aubergines, trimmed and quartered
1 tsp salt
2 tbsp sunflower oil
4 shallots, peeled and halved or quartered if large
2 garlic cloves, peeled and sliced
2 tbsp Thai green curry paste
150 ml/¼ pint chicken stock
1 tbsp Thai fish sauce
1 tbsp lemon juice

350 g/12 oz boneless, skinless turkey breast, cubed
1 red pepper, deseeded and sliced
125 g/4 oz French beans, trimmed and halved
25 g/1 oz creamed coconut
freshly boiled rice or steamed Thai fragrant rice, to serve

1 Place the aubergines into a colander and sprinkle with the salt. Set over a plate or in the sink to drain and leave for 30 minutes. Rinse under cold running water and pat dry on absorbent kitchen paper.

2 Heat a wok or large frying pan, add the sunflower oil and when hot, add the shallots and garlic and stir-fry for 3 minutes, or until beginning to brown. Add the curry paste and stir-fry for 1–2 minutes. Pour in the stock, fish sauce and lemon juice and simmer for 10 minutes.

3 Add the turkey, red pepper and French beans to the wok with the aubergines. Return to the boil, then simmer for 10–15 minutes, or until the turkey and vegetables are tender. Add the creamed coconut and stir until melted and the sauce has thickened. Turn into a warmed serving dish and serve immediately with rice.

FOOD FACT

Several types of aubergine are grown in Thailand. Generally the Thais prefer the small thin varieties, which have a more delicate flavour. You may find these in Oriental shops labelled as Chinese aubergines, but if you are unable to find them use baby aubergines as suggested here.

THAI CHICKEN WITH CHILLI & PEANUTS

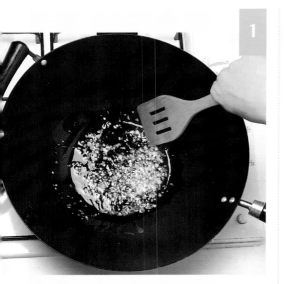

INGREDIENTS   Serves 4

2 tbsp vegetable or
  groundnut oil
1 garlic clove, peeled and
  finely chopped
1 tsp dried chilli flakes
350 g/12 oz boneless, skinless
  chicken breast, finely sliced
1 tbsp Thai fish sauce
2 tbsp peanuts, roasted and
  roughly chopped

225 g/ 8 oz sugar snap peas
3 tbsp chicken stock
1 tbsp light soy sauce
1 tbsp dark soy sauce
large pinch of sugar
freshly chopped coriander, to
  garnish
boiled or steamed rice, to
  serve

1 Heat a wok or large frying pan, add the oil and when hot, carefully swirl the oil around the wok until the sides are lightly coated with the oil. Add the garlic and stir-fry for 10–20 seconds, or until starting to brown. Add the chilli flakes and stir-fry for a few seconds more.

2 Add the finely sliced chicken to the wok and stir-fry for 2–3 minutes, or until the chicken has turned white.

3 Add the following ingredients, stirring well after each addition: fish sauce, peanuts, sugar snap peas, chicken stock, light and dark soy sauces and sugar. Give a final stir.

4 Bring the contents of the wok to the boil, then simmer gently for 3–4 minutes, or until the chicken and vegetables are tender. Remove from the heat and tip into a warmed serving dish. Garnish with chopped coriander and serve immediately with boiled or steamed rice.

FOOD FACT

Groundnut or peanut oil is also known as arachide oil. It is often used in Thai cuisine because it is mild and almost flavourless and can be heated to a very high temperature without burning, which makes it perfect for stir-frying and deep-frying. Do not be tempted to stir-fry with olive oil as it does not perform well. Using extra-virgin olive oil would be extremely wasteful as the delicate flavour of the oil would be destroyed.

THAI STIR-FRIED SPICY TURKEY

INGREDIENTS — Serves 4

2 tbsp Thai fragrant rice
2 tbsp lemon juice
3–5 tbsp chicken stock
2 tbsp Thai fish sauce
½–1 tsp cayenne pepper, or to taste
125 g/4 oz fresh turkey mince
2 shallots, peeled and chopped

½ lemon grass stalk, outer leaves discarded and finely sliced
1 lime leaf, finely sliced
1 spring onion, trimmed and finely chopped
freshly chopped coriander, to garnish
Chinese leaves, to serve

1 Place the rice in a small frying pan and cook, stirring constantly, over a medium high heat for 4–5 minutes, or until the rice is browned. Transfer to a spice grinder or blender and pulse briefly until roughly ground. Reserve.

2 Place the lemon juice, 3 tablespoons of the stock, the fish sauce and cayenne pepper into a small saucepan and bring to the boil. Add the turkey mince and return to the boil. Continue cooking over a high heat until the turkey is sealed all over.

3 Add the shallots to the saucepan with the lemon grass, lime leaf, spring onion and reserved rice. Continue cooking for another 1–2 minutes, or until the turkey is cooked through, adding a little more stock, if necessary to keep the mixture moist.

4 Spoon a little of the mixture into each Chinese leaf and arrange on a serving dish or individual plates. Garnish with a little chopped coriander and serve immediately.

TASTY TIP

Cooking the rice before grinding, gives it a nutty, toasted flavour. Take care to only cook it until lightly browned and not at all blackened, as this would spoil the flavour. Chinese leaves make great serving containers and enable this dish to be eaten with fingers. It would also make a delicious starter for 6 to 8 people.

HOT-&-SOUR DUCK

INGREDIENTS   Serves 4

4 small boneless duck breasts,
  with skin on, thinly sliced on
  the diagonal
1 tsp salt
4 tbsp tamarind pulp
4 shallots, peeled and
  chopped
2 garlic cloves, peeled and
  chopped
2.5 cm/1 inch piece fresh root
  ginger, chopped
1 tsp ground coriander

3 large red chillies, deseeded
  and chopped
½ tsp turmeric
6 blanched almonds, chopped
125 ml/4 fl oz vegetable oil
227 g can bamboo shoots,
  drained, rinsed and finely
  sliced
salt and freshly ground black
  pepper
sprigs of fresh coriander, to
  garnish
freshly cooked rice, to serve

1 Sprinkle the duck with the salt, cover lightly and refrigerate for 20 minutes.

2 Meanwhile, place the tamarind pulp in a small bowl, pour over 4 tablespoons of hot water and leave for 2–3 minutes or until softened. Press the mixture through a sieve into another bowl to produce about 2 tablespoons of smooth juice.

3 Place the tamarind juice in a food processor with the shallots, garlic, ginger, coriander, chillies, turmeric and almonds. Blend until smooth, adding a little more hot water if necessary, and reserve the paste.

4 Heat a wok or large frying pan, add the oil and when hot, stir-fry the duck in batches for about 3 minutes, or until just

coloured, then drain on absorbent kitchen paper.

5 Discard all but 2 tablespoons of the oil in the wok. Return to the heat. Add the paste and stir-fry for 5 minutes. Add the duck and stir-fry for 2 minutes. Add the bamboo shoots and stir-fry for 2 minutes. Season to taste with salt and pepper. Turn into a warmed serving dish, garnish with a sprig of fresh coriander and serve immediately with rice.

FOOD FACT

Although bamboo shoots are virtually flavourless, they add a fresh flavour and crunchiness to dishes. Occasionally, they can be bought fresh, but the canned version is inexpensive and almost as good.

THAI CHICKEN FRIED RICE

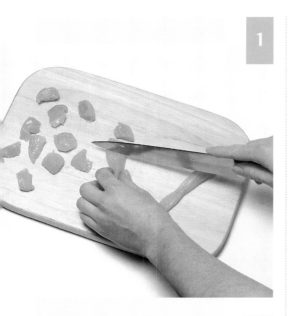

INGREDIENTS

Serves 4

175 g/6 oz boneless, chicken breast
2 tbsp vegetable oil
2 garlic cloves, peeled and finely chopped
2 tsp medium curry paste
450 g/1 lb cold cooked rice
1 tbsp light soy sauce
2 tbsp Thai fish sauce

large pinch of sugar
freshly ground black pepper

TO GARNISH:
2 spring onions, trimmed and shredded lengthways
½ small onion, peeled and very finely sliced

1 Using a sharp knife, trim the chicken, discarding any sinew or fat and cut into small cubes. Reserve.

2 Heat a wok or large frying pan, add the oil and when hot, add the garlic and cook for 10–20 seconds or until just golden. Add the curry paste and stir-fry for a few seconds. Add the chicken and stir-fry for 3–4 minutes, or until tender and the chicken has turned white.

3 Stir the cold cooked rice into the chicken mixture, then add the soy sauce, fish sauce and sugar, stirring well after each addition. Stir-fry for 2–3 minutes, or until the chicken is cooked through and the rice is piping hot.

4 Check the seasoning and, if necessary, add a little extra soy sauce. Turn the rice and chicken mixture into a warmed serving dish. Season lightly with black pepper and garnish with shredded spring onion and onion slices. Serve immediately.

TASTY TIP

There is a huge range of curry pastes available, from mild and only slightly spicy to burning hot. Although a medium one has been suggested for this dish, you can, of course, use your favourite, but do choose a Thai curry paste, such as red or green curry paste, rather than an Indian-style one.

WARM NOODLE SALAD WITH SESAME & PEANUT DRESSING

INGREDIENTS
Serves 4–6

125 g/4 oz smooth peanut butter

6 tbsp sesame oil

3 tbsp light soy sauce

2 tbsp red wine vinegar

1 tbsp freshly grated root ginger

2 tbsp double cream

250 g pack Chinese fine egg noodles

125 g/4 oz beansprouts

225 g/8 oz baby sweetcorn

125 g/4 oz carrots, peeled and cut into matchsticks

125 g/4 oz mangetout

125 g/4 oz cucumber, cut into thin strips

3 spring onions, trimmed and finely shredded

1 Place the peanut butter, 4 tablespoons of the sesame oil, the soy sauce, vinegar and ginger in a food processor. Blend until smooth, then stir in 75 ml/3 fl oz hot water and blend again. Pour in the cream, blend briefly until smooth. Pour the dressing into a jug and reserve.

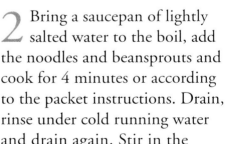

2 Bring a saucepan of lightly salted water to the boil, add the noodles and beansprouts and cook for 4 minutes or according to the packet instructions. Drain, rinse under cold running water and drain again. Stir in the remaining sesame oil and keep warm.

3 Bring a saucepan of lightly salted water to the boil and add the baby sweetcorn, carrots and mangetout and cook for 3–4 minutes, or until just tender but still crisp. Drain and cut the mangetout in half. Slice the baby sweetcorn (if very large) into 2–3 pieces and arrange on a warmed serving dish with the noodles. Add the cucumber strips and spring onions. Spoon over a little of the dressing and serve immediately with the remaining dressing.

FOOD FACT

There are 2 types of sesame oil. A light and pale one made from untoasted seeds; the other dark and rich. Its wonderfully nutty aroma and flavour is too overpowering to use in large quantities, so choose a light version for this recipe. Alternatively, blend 2 tablespoons of dark toasted sesame oil with 4 tablespoons of a milder oil such as groundnut or sunflower.

SPICY CUCUMBER STIR FRY

INGREDIENTS   Serves 4

25 g/1 oz black soya beans,
  soaked in cold water,
  overnight
1½ cucumbers
2 tsp salt
1 tbsp groundnut oil
½ tsp mild chilli powder

4 garlic cloves, peeled and
  crushed
5 tbsp chicken stock
1 tsp sesame oil
1 tbsp freshly chopped
  parsley, to garnish

1 Rinse the soaked beans thoroughly, then drain. Place in a saucepan, cover with cold water and bring to the boil, skimming off any scum that rises to the surface. Boil for 10 minutes, then reduce the heat and simmer for 1–1½ hours. Drain and reserve.

2 Peel the cucumbers, slice lengthways and remove the seeds. Cut into 2.5 cm/1 inch slices and place in a colander over a bowl. Sprinkle the salt over the cucumber and leave for 30 minutes. Rinse thoroughly in cold water, drain and pat dry with absorbent kitchen paper.

3 Heat a wok or large frying pan, add the oil and when hot, add the chilli powder, garlic and black beans and stir-fry for 30 seconds. Add the cucumber and stir-fry for 20 seconds.

4 Pour the stock into the wok and cook for 3–4 minutes, or until the cucumber is very tender. The liquid will have evaporated at this stage. Remove from the heat and stir in the sesame oil. Turn into a warmed serving dish, garnish with chopped parsley and serve immediately.

FOOD FACT

Black soya beans are small oval beans that are referred to as 'meat of the earth' in China, where they were once considered sacred. Soya beans are the only pulse that contains all 8 essential amino acids, so they are an excellent source of protein. They are extremely dense and need to be soaked for at least 5 hours before cooking. Rinse after soaking, place in a saucepan, cover with cold water and bring to the boil. Boil vigorously for 10 minutes, removing any scum that rises to the surface. Drain, rinse again, then re-cover in cold water. Bring to the boil, cover and simmer for 1–1½ hours or until tender.

CHINESE EGG FRIED RICE

INGREDIENTS
Serves 4

250 g/9 oz long-grain rice
1 tbsp dark sesame oil
2 large eggs
1 tbsp sunflower oil
2 garlic cloves, peeled and
  crushed
2.5 cm/1 inch piece fresh root
  ginger, peeled and grated
1 carrot, peeled and cut into
  matchsticks
125 g/4 oz mangetout, halved

220 g can water chestnuts,
  drained and halved
1 yellow pepper, deseeded
  and diced
4 spring onions, trimmed and
  finely shredded
2 tbsp light soy sauce
½ tsp paprika
salt and freshly ground black
  pepper

1 Bring a saucepan of lightly salted water to the boil, add the rice and cook for 15 minutes or according to the packet instructions. Drain and leave to cool.

2 Heat a wok or large frying pan and add the sesame oil. Beat the eggs in a small bowl and pour into the hot wok. Using a fork, draw the egg in from the sides of the pan to the centre until it sets, then turn over and cook the other side. When set and golden turn out on to a board. Leave to cool, then cut into very thin strips.

3 Wipe the wok clean with absorbent kitchen paper, return to the heat and add the sunflower oil. When hot add the garlic and ginger and stir-fry for 30 seconds. Add the remaining vegetables and continue to

stir-fry for 3–4 minutes, or until tender but still crisp.

4 Stir the reserved cooked rice into the wok with the soy sauce and paprika and season to taste with salt and pepper. Fold in the cooked egg strips and heat through. Tip into a warmed serving dish and serve immediately.

HELPFUL HINT

Fried rice was originally devised as a tasty way of using leftover rice. The finest is made from recently cooked rice that is cool, but has not been kept in a refrigerator, which means that it is neither too damp or too dry. Here the rice is subtly spiced with garlic and ginger. Do not store cooked rice for longer than 24 hours.

VEGETABLE TEMPURA

INGREDIENTS

Serves 4–6

125 g/4 oz rice flour
75 g/3 oz plain flour
4 tsp baking powder
1 tbsp dried mustard powder
2 tsp semolina
salt and freshly ground black
   pepper
300 ml/½ pint groundnut oil
125 g/4 oz courgette, trimmed
   and thickly sliced

125 g/4 oz mangetout
125 g/4 oz baby sweetcorn
4 small red onions, peeled and
   quartered
1 large red pepper, deseeded
   and cut into 2.5 cm/1 inch
   wide strips
light soy sauce, to serve

1 Sift the rice flour and the plain flour into a large bowl, then sift in the baking powder and dried mustard powder.

2 Stir the semolina into the flour mixture and season to taste with salt and pepper. Gradually beat in 300 ml/½ pint cold water to produce a thin coating batter. Leave to stand at room temperature for 30 minutes.

3 Heat a wok or large frying pan, add the oil and heat to 180°C/350°F. Working in batches and using a slotted spoon, dip the vegetables in the batter until well coated, then drop them carefully into the hot oil. Cook each batch for 2–3 minutes or until golden. Drain on absorbent kitchen paper and keep warm while cooking the remaining batches.

4 Transfer the vegetables to a warmed serving platter and serve immediately with the light soy sauce to use as a dipping sauce.

HELPFUL HINT

The batter for these deep-fried vegetable fritters should be very thin, so that you can see-through it after cooking. When making take care not to overmix; the batter should remain slightly lumpy. Deep-fry just a few at a time, otherwise the temperature of the oil will drop and the fritters will not be crisp.

THAI-STYLE CAULIFLOWER & POTATO CURRY

INGREDIENTS   Serves 4

450 g/1 lb new potatoes, peeled and halved or quartered

350 g/12 oz cauliflower florets

3 garlic cloves, peeled and crushed

1 onion, peeled and finely chopped

40 g/1½ oz ground almonds

1 tsp ground coriander

½ tsp ground cumin

½ tsp turmeric

3 tbsp groundnut oil

salt and freshly ground black pepper

50 g/2 oz creamed coconut, broken into small pieces

200 ml/7 fl oz vegetable stock

1 tbsp mango chutney

sprigs of fresh coriander, to garnish

freshly cooked long-grain rice, to serve

1 Bring a saucepan of lightly salted water to the boil, add the potatoes and cook for 15 minutes or until just tender. Drain and leave to cool. Boil the cauliflower for 2 minutes, then drain and refresh under cold running water. Drain again and reserve.

2 Meanwhile, blend the garlic, onion, ground almonds and spices with 2 tablespoons of the oil and salt and pepper to taste in a food processor until a smooth paste is formed. Heat a wok, add the remaining oil and when hot, add the spice paste and cook for 3–4 minutes, stirring continuously.

3 Dissolve the creamed coconut in 6 tablespoons of boiling water and add to the wok. Pour in the stock, cook for 2–3 minutes, then stir in the cooked potatoes and cauliflower.

4 Stir in the mango chutney and heat through for 3–4 minutes or until piping hot. Tip into a warmed serving dish, garnish with sprigs of fresh coriander and serve immediately with freshly cooked rice.

HELPFUL HINT

Mildly flavoured vegetables absorb the taste and colour of spices in this dish. Take care not to overcook the cauliflower; it should be only just tender for this dish. Broccoli florets would make a good alternative.

COCONUT-BAKED COURGETTES

INGREDIENTS   Serves 4

3 tbsp groundnut oil
1 onion, peeled and finely
  sliced
4 garlic cloves, peeled and
  crushed
½ tsp chilli powder
1 tsp ground coriander
6–8 tbsp desiccated coconut
1 tbsp tomato purée

700 g/1½ lb courgettes, thinly
  sliced
freshly chopped parsley, to
  garnish

1 Preheat the oven to 180°C/350°F/Gas Mark 4, 10 minutes before cooking. Lightly oil a 1.4 litre/2½ pint ovenproof gratin dish. Heat a wok, add the oil and when hot, add the onion and stir-fry for 2–3 minutes or until softened. Add the garlic, chilli powder and coriander and stir-fry for 1–2 minutes.

2 Pour 300 ml/½ pint cold water into the wok and bring to the boil. Add the coconut and tomato purée and simmer for 3–4 minutes; most of the water will evaporate at this stage. Spoon 4 tablespoons of the spice and coconut mixture into a small bowl and reserve.

3 Stir the courgettes into the remaining spice and coconut mixture, coating well. Spoon the courgettes into the oiled gratin dish and sprinkle the reserved spice and coconut mixture evenly over the top. Bake, uncovered, in the preheated oven for 15–20 minutes, or until golden. Garnish with chopped parsley and serve immediately.

HELPFUL HINT

Because coconut is high in fat, desiccated coconut has a relatively short shelf-life. Unless you use it in large quantities, buy it in small packets, checking the sell-by date. Once opened, desiccated coconut should be used within 2 months. You can also buy it from Asian grocers, but as there is often no sell-by date, smell the contents; it is easy to detect rancid coconut.

COOKED VEGETABLE SALAD WITH SATAY SAUCE

INGREDIENTS   Serves 4

125 ml/4 fl oz groundnut oil
225 g/8 oz unsalted peanuts
1 onion, peeled and finely
  chopped
1 garlic clove, peeled and
  crushed
½ tsp chilli powder
1 tsp ground coriander
½ tsp ground cumin
½ tsp sugar
1 tbsp dark soy sauce
2 tbsp fresh lemon juice
2 tbsp light olive oil
salt and freshly ground black
  pepper

125 g/4 oz French green
  beans, trimmed and halved
125 g/4 oz carrots
125 g/4 oz cauliflower florets
125 g/4 oz broccoli florets
125 g/4 oz Chinese leaves or
  pak choi, trimmed and
  shredded
125 g/4 oz beansprouts
1 tbsp sesame oil

TO GARNISH:

sprigs of fresh watercress
cucumber, cut into slivers

1 Heat a wok, add the oil, and when hot, add the peanuts and stir-fry for 3–4 minutes. Drain on absorbent kitchen paper and leave to cool. Blend in a food processor to a fine powder.

2 Place the onion and garlic, with the spices, sugar, soy sauce, lemon juice and olive oil in a food processor. Season to taste with salt and pepper, then process into a paste. Transfer to a wok and stir-fry for 3–4 minutes.

3 Stir 600 ml/1 pint hot water into the paste and bring to the boil. Add the ground peanuts and simmer gently for 5–6 minutes or until the mixture thickens. Reserve the satay sauce.

4 Cook in batches in lightly salted boiling water. Cook the French beans, carrots, cauliflower and broccoli for 3–4 minutes, and the Chinese leaves or pak choi and beansprouts for 2 minutes. Drain each batch, drizzle over the sesame oil and arrange on a large warmed serving dish. Garnish with watercress sprigs and cucumber. Serve with the satay sauce.

FOOD FACT

Peanuts are not actually nuts, but a member of the pea family that grow underground. They are highly nutritious.

MIXED VEGETABLES STIR FRY

INGREDIENTS

Serves 4

2 tbsp groundnut oil
4 garlic cloves, peeled and
finely sliced
2.5 cm/1 inch piece fresh root
ginger, peeled and finely
sliced
75 g/3 oz broccoli florets
50 g/2 oz mangetout, trimmed
75 g/3 oz carrots, peeled and
cut into matchsticks
1 green pepper, deseeded and
cut into strips
1 red pepper, deseeded and
cut into strips
1 tbsp soy sauce

1 tbsp hoisin sauce
1 tsp sugar
salt and freshly ground black
pepper
4 spring onions, trimmed and
shredded, to garnish

1 Heat a wok, add the oil and when hot, add the garlic and ginger slices and stir-fry for 1 minute.

2 Add the broccoli florets to the wok, stir-fry for 1 minute, then add the mangetout, carrots and the green and red peppers and stir-fry for a further 3–4 minutes, or until tender but still crisp.

3 Blend the soy sauce, hoisin sauce and sugar in a small bowl. Stir well, season to taste with salt and pepper and pour into the wok. Transfer the vegetables to a warmed serving dish. Garnish with shredded spring onions and serve immediately with a selection of other Thai dishes.

FOOD FACT

Hoisin sauce is a thick, dark brownish red sauce, made by blending soya beans with sugar, vinegar and spices. It has a spicy, sweetish taste and is often used in southern Chinese cooking. It may also be served as a sauce for Peking duck instead of the more traditional sweet bean sauce.

HELPFUL HINT

Vary the combination of vegetables – try asparagus spears cut into short lengths, sliced mushroons, French beans, red onion wedges and cauliflower florets.

THAI STUFFED EGGS WITH SPINACH & SESAME SEEDS

INGREDIENTS   Makes 8

4 large eggs
salt and freshly ground black
   pepper
225 g/8 oz baby spinach
2 garlic cloves, peeled and
   crushed
1 tbsp spring onions, trimmed
   and finely chopped
1 tbsp sesame seeds

75 g/3 oz plain flour
1 tbsp light olive oil
300 ml/½ pint vegetable oil for
   frying

TO GARNISH:
sliced red chilli
snipped fresh chives

1 Bring a small saucepan of water to the boil, add the eggs, bring back to the boil and cook for 6–7 minutes. Plunge into cold water, then shell and cut in half lengthways. Using a teaspoon, remove the yolks and place in a bowl. Reserve the whites.

2 Place 1 teaspoon of water and ½ teaspoon of salt in a saucepan, add the spinach and cook until tender and wilted. Drain, squeeze out the excess moisture and chop. Mix with the egg yolk, then stir in the garlic, spring onions and sesame seeds. Season to taste with salt and pepper. Fill the egg shells with the mixture, smoothing into a mound.

3 Place the flour in a bowl with the olive oil, a large pinch of salt and 125 ml/4 fl oz warm water. Beat together to make completely smooth batter.

4 Heat a wok, add the vegetable oil and heat to 180°C/350°F. Dip the stuffed eggs in the batter, allowing any excess batter to drip back into the bowl, and deep-fry in batches for 3–4 minutes or until golden brown. Place the eggs in the wok filled side down first, then turn over to finish cooking. Remove from the wok with a slotted spoon and drain on absorbent kitchen paper. Serve hot or cold garnished with snipped chives and chilli rings.

HELPFUL HINT

Eggs are often stuffed with a combination of pork and crabmeat, but this vegetarian version makes a delicious alternative. They can be made up to 24 hours ahead of serving.

SAVOURY WONTONS

INGREDIENTS

Makes 15

125 g/4 oz filo pastry or
  wonton skins
15 whole chive leaves
225 g/8 oz spinach
25 g/1 oz butter
½ tsp salt
225 g/8 oz mushrooms, wiped
  and roughly chopped
1 garlic clove, peeled and
  crushed
1–2 tbsp dark soy sauce
2.5 cm/1 inch piece fresh root
  ginger, peeled and grated

salt and freshly ground black
  pepper
1 small egg, beaten
300 ml/½ pint groundnut oil for
  deep-frying

TO GARNISH:
spring onion curls
radish roses

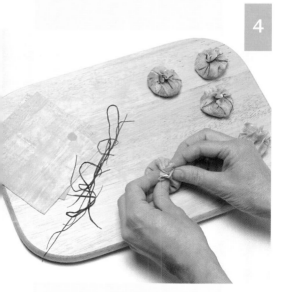

1 Cut the filo pastry or wonton skins into 12.5 cm/5 inch squares, stack and cover with clingfilm. Chill in the refrigerator while preparing the filling. Blanch the chive leaves in boiling water for 1 minute, drain and reserve.

2 Melt the butter in a saucepan, add the spinach and salt and cook for 2–3 minutes or until wilted. Add the mushrooms and garlic and cook for 2–3 minutes or until tender.

3 Transfer the spinach and mushroom mixture to a bowl. Stir in the soy sauce and ginger. Season to taste with salt and pepper.

4 Place a small spoonful of the spinach and mushroom mixture on to a pastry or wonton square and brush the edges with

beaten egg. Gather up the 4 corners to make a little bag and tie with a chive leaf. Make up the remainder of the wontons.

5 Heat a wok, add the oil and heat to 180°C/350°F. Deep-fry the wontons in batches for 2–3 minutes, or until golden and crisp. Drain on absorbent kitchen paper and serve immediately, garnished with spring onion curls and radish roses.

HELPFUL HINT

It is important to cover the filo pastry squares or wonton skins you are not immediately working with in clingfilm, to prevent them from drying out.

CORN FRITTERS WITH HOT & SPICY RELISH

INGREDIENTS   Makes 16–20

325 g can sweetcorn kernels,
    drained
1 onion, peeled and very finely
    chopped
1 spring onion, trimmed and
    very finely chopped
½ tsp chilli powder
1 tsp ground coriander
4 tbsp plain flour
1 tsp baking powder
1 medium egg
salt and freshly ground black
    pepper

300 ml/½ pint groundnut oil
sprigs of fresh coriander, to
    garnish

FOR THE SPICY RELISH:
3 tbsp sunflower oil
1 onion, peeled and very finely
    chopped
¼ tsp dried crushed chillies
2 garlic cloves, peeled and
    crushed
2 tbsp plum sauce

1 Make the relish. Heat a wok, add the sunflower oil and when hot, add the onion and stir-fry for 3–4 minutes or until softened. Add the chillies and garlic, stir-fry for 1 minute, then leave to cool slightly. Stir in the plum sauce, transfer to a food processor and blend until the consistency of chutney. Reserve.

2 Place the sweetcorn into a food processor and blend briefly until just mashed. Transfer to a bowl with the onions, chilli powder, coriander, flour, baking powder and egg. Season to taste with salt and pepper and mix together.

3 Heat a wok, add the oil and heat to 180°C/350°F. Working in batches, drop a few spoonfuls of the sweetcorn mixture into the oil and deep-fry for 3–4 minutes, or until golden and crispy, turning occasionally. Using a slotted spoon, remove and drain on absorbent kitchen paper. Arrange on a warmed serving platter, garnish with sprigs of coriander and serve immediately with the relish.

TASTY TIP

To make the dish a more traditional way, brush 2 cobs of fresh sweetcorn with groundnut oil and grill for 7–8 minutes, or until the kernels are beginning to brown. When the cobs are cool enough to handle, cut off the kernels.

CHINESE LEAVES WITH SWEET-&-SOUR SAUCE

INGREDIENTS   Serves 4

1 head Chinese leaves	3 tbsp orange juice
200 g pack pak choi	2 tbsp tomato purée
1 tbsp cornflour	3 tbsp sunflower oil
1 tbsp soy sauce	15 g/½ oz butter
2 tbsp brown sugar	1 tsp salt
3 tbsp red wine vinegar	2 tbsp toasted sesame seeds

1 Discard any tough outer leaves and stalks from the Chinese leaves and pak choi and wash well. Drain thoroughly and pat dry with absorbent kitchen paper. Shred the Chinese leaves and pak choi lengthways. Reserve.

2 In a small bowl, blend the cornflour with 4 tablespoons of water. Add the soy sauce, sugar, vinegar, orange juice and tomato purée and stir until blended thoroughly.

3 Pour the sauce into a small saucepan and bring to the boil. Simmer gently for 2–3 minutes, or until the sauce is thickened and smooth.

4 Meanwhile, heat a wok or large frying pan and add the sunflower oil and butter. When melted, add the prepared Chinese leaves and pak choi, sprinkle with the salt and stir-fry for 2 minutes. Reduce the heat and cook gently for a further 1–2 minutes or until tender.

5 Transfer the Chinese leaves and pak choi to a warmed serving platter and drizzle over the warm sauce. Sprinkle with the toasted sesame seeds and serve immediately.

FOOD FACT

Chinese leaves have a mild, delicate, faintly cabbage-like flavour. They have pale, tightly wrapped crinkly leaves and crisp white stems. Because they are now grown in and imported from Spain, Holland and Israel, they are available all-year round. They will keep for at least a week in the salad drawer of the refrigerator.

BEAN & CASHEW STIR FRY

INGREDIENTS   Serves 4

3 tbsp sunflower oil
1 onion, peeled and finely
  chopped
1 celery stalk, trimmed and
  chopped
2.5 cm/1 inch piece fresh root
  ginger, peeled and grated
2 garlic cloves, peeled and
  crushed
1 red chilli, deseeded and
  finely chopped
175 g/6 oz fine French beans,
  trimmed and halved

175 g/6 oz mangetout, sliced
  diagonally into 3
75 g/3 oz unsalted cashew
  nuts
1 tsp brown sugar
125 ml/4 fl oz vegetable stock
2 tbsp dry sherry
1 tbsp light soy sauce
1 tsp red wine vinegar
salt and freshly ground black
  pepper
freshly chopped coriander, to
  garnish

1 Heat a wok or large frying pan, add the oil and when hot, add the onion and celery and stir-fry gently for 3–4 minutes or until softened.

2 Add the ginger, garlic and chilli to the wok and stir-fry for 30 seconds. Stir in the French beans and mangetout together with the cashew nuts and continue to stir-fry for 1–2 minutes, or until the nuts are golden brown.

3 Dissolve the sugar in the stock, then blend with the sherry, soy sauce and vinegar. Stir into the bean mixture and bring to the boil. Simmer gently, stirring occasionally for 3–4 minutes, or until the beans and mangetout are tender but still crisp and the sauce has thickened slightly. Season to taste with salt

and pepper. Transfer to a warmed serving bowl or spoon on to individual plates. Sprinkle with freshly chopped coriander and serve immediately.

FOOD FACT

Spicy and warm, fresh coriander features frequently in Chinese and especially Thai dishes. It has a similar appearance to flat leaf parsley, but the flavour is completely different. It is often sold with its roots intact and these are sometimes used in Thai curry pastes as they have a much more intense flavour than the leaves.

FRIED RICE WITH BAMBOO SHOOTS & GINGER

INGREDIENTS

Serves 4

4 tbsp sunflower oil
1 onion, peeled and finely chopped
225 g/8 oz long-grain rice
3 garlic cloves, peeled and cut into slivers
2.5 cm/1 inch piece fresh root ginger, peeled and grated
3 spring onions, trimmed and chopped
450 ml/¾ pint vegetable stock

125 g/4 oz button mushrooms, wiped and halved
75 g/3 oz frozen peas, thawed
2 tbsp light soy sauce
500 g can bamboo shoots, drained and thinly sliced
salt and freshly ground black pepper
cayenne pepper, to taste
fresh coriander leaves, to garnish

1 Heat a wok, add the oil and when hot, add the onion and cook gently for 3–4 minutes, then add the long-grain rice and cook for 3–4 minutes or until golden, stirring frequently.

2 Add the garlic, ginger and chopped spring onions to the wok and stir well. Pour the chicken stock into a small saucepan and bring to the boil. Carefully ladle the hot stock into the wok, stir well, then simmer gently for 10 minutes or until most of the liquid has been absorbed.

3 Stir the button mushrooms, peas and soy sauce into the wok and continue to cook for a further 5 minutes, or until the rice is tender, adding a little extra stock if necessary.

4 Add the bamboo shoots to the wok and carefully stir in. Season to taste with salt, pepper and cayenne pepper. Cook for 2–3 minutes or until heated through. Tip on to a warmed serving dish, garnish with coriander leaves and serve immediately.

FOOD FACT

Button, cap and flat mushrooms are actually the same type of mushroom but in different stages of maturity. The button mushroom is the youngest and therefore has the mildest flavour. Brown-capped chestnut mushrooms, which look similar but have a richer, nutty flavour could also be used here.

SPRING ROLLS WITH MIXED VEGETABLES

INGREDIENTS

Makes 12

2 tbsp sesame oil

125 g/4 oz broccoli florets, cut into small pieces

125 g/4 oz carrots, peeled and cut into matchsticks

125 g/4 oz courgettes, cut into strips

150 g/5 oz button mushrooms, finely chopped

2.5 cm/1 inch piece fresh root ginger, peeled and grated

1 garlic clove, peeled and finely chopped

4 spring onions, trimmed and finely chopped

75 g/3 oz beansprouts

1 tbsp light soy sauce

pinch of cayenne pepper

4 tbsp plain flour

12 sheets filo pastry

300 ml/½ pint groundnut oil

spring onion curls, to garnish

1 Heat a wok, add the sesame oil and when hot, add the broccoli, carrots, courgettes, mushrooms, ginger, garlic and spring onions and stir-fry for 1–2 minutes, or until slightly softened.

2 Turn into a bowl, add the beansprouts, soy sauce and cayenne pepper and mix together. Transfer the vegetables to a colander and drain for 5 minutes. Meanwhile, blend the flour with 2–3 tablespoons of water to form a paste and reserve.

3 Fold a sheet of filo pastry in half and in half again, brushing a little water between each layer. Place a spoonful of the drained vegetable mixture on the pastry. Brush a little of the flour paste along the edges. Turn the edges into the centre, then roll up and seal. Repeat with the rest.

4 Wipe the wok clean, return to the heat, add the oil and heat to 190°C/375°F. Add the spring rolls in batches and deep-fry for 2–3 minutes, or until golden. Drain on absorbent kitchen paper, arrange on a platter, garnish with spring onion curls and serve immediately.

TASTY TIP

For a lower-fat version of this dish, you can bake the spring rolls. Lightly brush them with groundnut oil, place on a baking sheet and cook on the centre shelf of a preheated oven at 190°C/375°F/Gas Mark 5 for 10 minutes, or until golden brown and crisp.

THAI CURRY WITH TOFU

INGREDIENTS   Serves 4

750 ml/1¼ pints coconut milk
700 g/1½ lb tofu, drained and
  cut into small cubes
salt and freshly ground black
  pepper
4 garlic cloves, peeled and
  chopped
1 large onion, peeled and cut
  into wedges
1 tsp crushed dried chillies
grated rind of 1 lemon
2.5 cm/1 inch piece fresh root
  ginger, peeled and grated

1 tbsp ground coriander
1 tsp ground cumin
1 tsp turmeric
2 tbsp light soy sauce
1 tsp cornflour
Thai fragrant rice, to serve

TO GARNISH:
2 red chillies, deseeded and
  cut into rings
1 tbsp freshly chopped
  coriander
lemon wedges

1 Pour 600 ml/1 pint of the coconut milk into a saucepan and bring to the boil. Add the tofu, season to taste with salt and pepper and simmer gently for 10 minutes. Using a slotted spoon, remove the tofu and place on a plate. Reserve the coconut milk.

2 Place the garlic, onion, dried chillies, lemon rind, ginger, spices and soy sauce in a blender or food processor and blend until a smooth paste is formed. Pour the remaining 150 ml/¼ pint coconut milk into a clean saucepan and whisk in the spicy paste. Cook, stirring continuously, for 15 minutes, or until the curry sauce is very thick.

3 Gradually whisk the reserved coconut milk into the curry and heat to simmering point. Add the cooked tofu and cook for 5–10 minutes. Blend the cornflour with 1 tablespoon of cold water and stir into the curry. Cook until thickened. Turn into a warmed serving dish and garnish with chilli, lemon wedges and coriander. Serve immediately with Thai fragrant rice.

FOOD FACT

Use firm tofu for this dish, whether plain, marinated or smoked, all of which are available from health food and Oriental shops. Simmer it very gently in the coconut milk, stirring only occasionally so that it does not break up. Firm tofu can be kept in the refrigerator for up to a week, if covered in water, which is changed every few days.

CHINESE OMELETTE

INGREDIENTS

Serves 1

50 g/2 oz beansprouts
50 g/2 oz carrots, peeled and
   cut into matchsticks
1 cm/½ inch piece fresh root
   ginger, peeled and grated
1 tsp soy sauce
2 large eggs
salt and freshly ground black
   pepper
1 tbsp dark sesame oil

TO SERVE:
tossed green salad
Special Fried Rice, (see page
   114)
soy sauce

1 Lightly rinse the beansprouts, then place in the top of a bamboo steamer with the carrots. Add the grated ginger and soy sauce. Set the steamer over a pan or wok half-filled with gently simmering water and steam for 10 minutes, or until the vegetables are tender but still crisp. Reserve and keep warm.

2 Whisk the eggs in a bowl until frothy and season to taste with salt and pepper. Heat a 20.5 cm/8 inch omelette or frying pan, add the sesame oil and when very hot, pour in the beaten eggs. Whisk the eggs around with a fork, then allow them to cook and start to set. When the top surface starts to bubble, tilt the edges to allow the uncooked egg to run underneath.

3 Spoon the beansprout and carrot mixture over the top of the omelette and allow it to cook a little longer. When it

has set, slide the omelette on to a warmed serving dish and carefully roll up. Serve immediately with a tossed green salad, special fried rice and extra soy sauce.

TASTY TIP

Vary the filling ingredients of this omelette with whatever vegetables you have in your refrigerator. Try sliced spring onions, fine strips of red or green peppers, mangetout halved lengthways, or a few green beans. Cut them into even sizes so that they are all tender at the same time.

CRISPY PANCAKE ROLLS

INGREDIENTS   Makes 8

250 g/9 oz plain flour
pinch of salt
1 medium egg
4 tsp sunflower oil
2 tbsp light olive oil
2 cm/¾ inch piece fresh root
  ginger, peeled and grated
1 garlic clove, peeled and
  crushed
225 g/8 oz tofu, drained and
  cut into small dice

2 tbsp soy sauce
1 tbsp dry sherry
175 g/6 oz button mushrooms,
  wiped and chopped
1 celery stalk, trimmed and
  finely chopped
2 spring onions, trimmed and
  finely chopped
2 tbsp groundnut oil
fresh coriander sprig and sliced
  spring onion, to garnish

1 Sift 225 g/8 oz of the flour with the salt into a large bowl, make a well in the centre and drop in the egg. Beat to form a smooth, thin batter, gradually adding 300 ml/½ pint of water and drawing in the flour from the sides of the bowl. Mix the remaining flour with 1–2 tablespoons of water to make a thick paste. Reserve.

2 Heat a little sunflower oil in a 20.5 cm/8 inch omelette or frying pan and pour in 2 tablespoons of the batter. Cook for 1–2 minutes, flip over and cook for a further 1–2 minutes, or until firm. Slide from the pan and keep warm. Make more pancakes with the remaining batter.

3 Heat a wok or large frying pan, add the olive oil and when hot, add the ginger, garlic and tofu, stir-fry for 30 seconds, then pour in the soy sauce and sherry. Add the mushrooms, celery and spring onions. Stir-fry for 1–2 minutes, then remove from the wok and leave to cool.

4 Place a little filling in the centre of each pancake. Brush the edges, with the flour paste, fold in the edges, then roll up into parcels. Heat the groundnut oil to 180°C/350°F in the wok. Fry the pancake rolls for 2–3 minutes or until golden. Serve immediately, garnished with chopped spring onions and a sprig of coriander.

HELPFUL HINT

The pancakes can be made up to 24 hours before they are needed. Place them in a single layer on a plate, cover with clingfilm and keep in the refrigerator. Leave them at room temperature for about 30 minutes before frying.

VEGETABLES IN COCONUT MILK WITH RICE NOODLES

INGREDIENTS

Serves 4

75 g/3 oz creamed coconut
1 tsp salt
2 tbsp sunflower oil
2 garlic cloves, peeled and finely chopped
2 red peppers, deseeded and cut into thin strips
2.5 cm/1 inch piece of fresh root ginger, peeled and cut into thin strips

125 g/4 oz baby sweetcorn
2 tsp cornflour
2 medium ripe but still firm avocados
1 small Cos lettuce, cut into thick strips
freshly cooked rice noodles, to serve

1 Roughly chop the creamed coconut, place in a bowl with the salt, then pour over 600 ml/1 pint of boiling water. Stir until the coconut has dissolved completely and reserve.

2 Heat a wok or large frying pan, add the oil and when hot, add the chopped garlic, sliced peppers and ginger. Cook for 30 seconds, then cover and cook very gently for 10 minutes or until the peppers are soft.

3 Pour in the reserved coconut milk and bring to the boil. Stir in the baby sweetcorn, cover and simmer for 5 minutes. Blend the cornflour with 2 teaspoons of water, pour into the wok and cook, stirring, for 2 minutes or until thickened slightly.

4 Cut the avocados in half, peel, remove the stone and slice. Add to the wok with the lettuce strips and stir until well mixed and heated through. Serve immediately on a bed of rice noodles.

FOOD FACT

Dried flat rice noodles, rice sticks and stir-fry rice noodles are all made from rice flour and come in varying thicknesses. Check on the packet for cooking instructions; they usually need to be soaked briefly in boiling water, about 2–3 minutes, or slightly longer in hot water.

THAI FRIED NOODLES

INGREDIENTS | Serves 4

450 g/1 lb tofu
2 tbsp dry sherry
125 g/4 oz medium egg
  noodles
125 g/4 oz mangetout, halved
3 tbsp groundnut oil
1 onion, peeled and finely
  sliced
1 garlic clove, peeled and
  finely sliced
2.5 cm/1 inch piece fresh root
  ginger, peeled and finely
  sliced

125 g/4 oz beansprouts
1 tbsp Thai fish sauce
2 tbsp light soy sauce
½ tsp sugar
salt and freshly ground black
  pepper
½ courgette, cut into
  matchsticks

TO GARNISH:
2 tbsp roasted peanuts,
  roughly chopped
sprigs of fresh basil

1 Cut the tofu into cubes and place in a bowl. Sprinkle over the sherry and toss to coat. Cover loosely and leave to marinate in the refrigerator for 30 minutes.

2 Bring a large saucepan of lightly salted water to the boil and add the noodles and mangetout. Simmer for 3 minutes or according to the packet instructions, then drain and rinse under cold running water. Leave to drain again.

3 Heat a wok or large frying pan, add the oil and when hot, add the onion and stir-fry for 2–3 minutes. Add the garlic and ginger and stir-fry for 30 seconds. Add the beansprouts and tofu, stir in the Thai fish sauce and the soy sauce with the sugar and season to taste with salt and pepper.

4 Stir-fry the tofu mixture over a medium heat for 2–3 minutes, then add the courgettes, noodles and mangetout and stir-fry for a further 1–2 minutes. Tip into a warmed serving dish or spoon on to individual plates. Sprinkle with the peanuts, add a sprig of basil and serve immediately.

FOOD FACT

One of the greatest assets of tofu is that it is virtually flavourless and can therefore be marinated in strong-tasting ingredients. Here it is gently tossed in sherry and added towards the end of cooking to retain the maximum amount of flavour.

CHICKEN & LAMB SATAY

INGREDIENTS   Makes 16

225 g/8 oz skinless, boneless
  chicken
225 g/8 oz lean lamb

FOR THE MARINADE:
1 small onion, peeled and
  finely chopped
2 garlic cloves, peeled and
  crushed
2.5 cm/1 inch piece fresh root
  ginger, peeled and grated
4 tbsp soy sauce
1 tsp ground coriander
2 tsp dark brown sugar
2 tbsp lime juice
1 tbsp vegetable oil

FOR THE PEANUT SAUCE:
300 ml/½ pint coconut milk
4 tbsp crunchy peanut butter
1 tbsp Thai fish sauce
1 tsp lime juice
1 tbsp chilli powder
1 tbsp brown sugar
salt and freshly ground black
  pepper

TO GARNISH:
sprigs of fresh coriander
lime wedges

1 Preheat the grill just before cooking. Soak the bamboo skewers for 30 minutes before required. Cut the chicken and lamb into thin strips, about 7.5 cm/3 inches long and place in 2 shallow dishes. Blend all the marinade ingredients together, then pour half over the chicken and half over the lamb. Stir until lightly coated, then cover with clingfilm and leave to marinate in the refrigerator for at least 2 hours, turning occasionally.

2 Remove the chicken and lamb from the marinade and thread on to the skewers. Reserve the marinade. Cook under the preheated grill for 8–10 minutes or until cooked, turning and brushing with the marinade.

3 Meanwhile, make the peanut sauce. Blend the coconut milk with the peanut butter, fish sauce, lime juice, chilli powder and sugar. Pour into a saucepan and cook gently for 5 minutes, stirring occasionally, then season to taste with salt and pepper. Garnish with coriander sprigs and lime wedges and serve the satays with the prepared sauce.

HELPFUL HINT

You can use metal skewers
for this dish, but bamboo
ones are more traditional and
they are inexpensive. Soaking
them in cold water prevents
them from scorching
during cooking.

SWEETCORN CAKES

INGREDIENTS   Serves 6–8

250 g/9 oz self-raising flour
3 tbsp Thai red curry paste
2 tbsp light soy sauce
2 tsp sugar
2 kaffir lime leaves, finely
   shredded
12 fine French beans,
   trimmed, finely chopped and
   blanched
340 g can sweetcorn, drained
salt and freshly ground black
   pepper
2 medium eggs

50 g/2 oz fresh white
   breadcrumbs
vegetable oil for deep-frying

FOR THE DIPPING SAUCE:
2 tbsp hoisin sauce
1 tbsp soft light brown sugar
1 tbsp sesame oil

TO SERVE:
halved cucumber slices
spring onions, sliced
   diagonally

1 Place the flour in a bowl, make a well in the centre, then add the curry paste, soy sauce and the sugar together with the shredded kaffir lime leaves, French beans and sweetcorn. Season to taste with salt and pepper, then beat 1 of the eggs and add to the mixture. Stir in with a fork adding 1–2 tablespoons of cold water to form a stiff dough. Knead lightly on a floured surface and form into a ball.

2 Divide the mixture into 16 pieces and shape into small balls, then flatten to form cakes about 1 cm/½ inch thick and 7.5 cm/3 inches in diameter. Beat the remaining egg and pour into a shallow dish. Dip the cakes first in a little beaten egg, then in the breadcrumbs until lightly coated.

3 Heat the oil in either a wok or deep-fat fryer to 180°C/350°F and deep-fry the cakes for 2–3 minutes or until golden brown in colour. Using a slotted spoon, remove and drain on absorbent kitchen paper.

4 Meanwhile, blend the hoisin sauce, sugar, 1 tablespoon of water and the sesame oil together until smooth and pour into a small bowl. Serve immediately with the sweetcorn cakes, cucumber and spring onions.

HELPFUL HINT

If you cannot get lime leaves, use 2 teaspoons of finely grated lime or lemon rind instead.

SOUR-&-SPICY PRAWN SOUP

INGREDIENTS

Serves 4

50 g/2 oz rice noodles
25 g/1 oz Chinese dried
  mushrooms
4 spring onions, trimmed
2 small green chillies
3 tbsp freshly chopped
  coriander
600 ml/1 pint chicken stock
2.5 cm/1 inch piece fresh root
  ginger, peeled and grated

2 lemon grass stalks, outer
  leaves discarded and finely
  chopped
4 kaffir lime leaves
12 raw king prawns, peeled
  with tail shell left on
2 tbsp Thai fish sauce
2 tbsp lime juice
salt and freshly ground black
  pepper

1 Place the noodles in cold water and leave to soak while preparing the soup. Place the dried mushrooms in a small bowl, cover with almost boiling water and leave for 20–30 minutes. Drain, strain and reserve the soaking liquor and discard any woody stems from the mushrooms.

2 Finely shred the spring onions and place into a small bowl. Cover with ice cold water and refrigerate until required and the spring onions have curled.

3 Place the green chillies with 2 tablespoons of the chopped coriander in a pestle and mortar and pound to a paste. Reserve.

4 Pour the stock into a saucepan and bring gently to the boil. Stir in the ginger, lemon grass and lime leaves with the reserved mushrooms and their liquor. Return to the boil.

5 Drain the noodles, add to the soup with the prawns, Thai fish sauce and lime juice and then stir in the chilli and coriander paste. Bring to the boil, then simmer for 3 minutes. Stir in the remaining chopped coriander and season to taste with salt and pepper. Ladle into warmed bowls sprinkle with the spring onions curls and serve immediately.

HELPFUL HINT

You will need about 150 ml/ ¼ pint of almost boiling water to cover the Chinese dried mushrooms. After soaking the mushrooms, rinse them under cold running water to remove any traces of grit. Also strain the soaking liquid through a very fine sieve or a piece of muslin before adding to the stock.

DIM SUM PORK PARCELS

INGREDIENTS

Makes about 40

125 g/4 oz canned water chestnuts, drained and finely chopped

125 g/4 oz raw prawns, peeled, deveined and coarsely chopped

350 g/12 oz fresh pork mince

2 tbsp smoked bacon, finely chopped

1 tbsp light soy sauce, plus extra, to serve

1 tsp dark soy sauce

1 tbsp Chinese rice wine

2 tbsp fresh root ginger, peeled and finely chopped

3 spring onions, trimmed and finely chopped

2 tsp sesame oil

1 medium egg white, lightly beaten

salt and freshly ground black pepper

2 tsp sugar

40 wonton skins, thawed if frozen

toasted sesame seeds, to garnish

soy sauce, to serve

1 Place the water chestnuts, prawns, pork mince and bacon in a bowl and mix together. Add the soy sauces, Chinese rice wine, ginger, chopped spring onion, sesame oil and egg white. Season to taste with salt and pepper, sprinkle in the sugar and mix the filling thoroughly.

2 Place a spoonful of filling in the centre of a wonton skin. Bring the sides up and press around the filling to make a basket shape. Flatten the base of the skin, so the wonton stands solid. The top should be wide open, exposing the filling.

3 Place the parcels on a heatproof plate, on a wire rack inside a wok or on the base of a muslin-lined bamboo steamer.

Place over a wok, half-filled with boiling water, cover, then steam the parcels for about 20 minutes. Do this in 2 batches. Transfer to a warmed serving plate, sprinkle with toasted sesame seeds, drizzle with soy sauce and serve immediately.

FOOD FACT

These steamed dumplings are known as *shao mai* in China, meaning 'cook and sell' and are a popular street food. Serve them with a choice of dips, such as a sweet chilli sauce or a mixture of finely grated ginger with a little clear honey, soy sauce, sesame oil and rice vinegar or dry sherry.

TURKEY WITH ORIENTAL MUSHROOMS

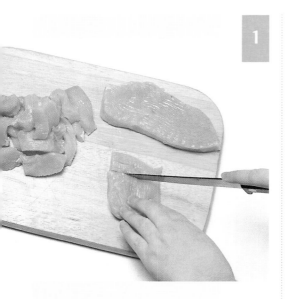

INGREDIENTS — Serves 4

15 g/½ oz dried Chinese mushrooms

450 g/1 lb turkey breast steaks

150 ml/¼ pint turkey or chicken stock

2 tbsp groundnut oil

1 red pepper, deseeded and sliced

225 g/8 oz sugar snap peas, trimmed

125 g/4 oz shiitake mushrooms, wiped and halved

125 g/4 oz oyster mushrooms, wiped and halved

2 tbsp yellow bean sauce

2 tbsp soy sauce

1 tbsp hot chilli sauce

freshly cooked noodles, to serve

1 Place the dried mushrooms in a small bowl, cover with almost boiling water and leave for 20–30 minutes. Drain and discard any woody stems from the mushrooms. Cut the turkey and into thin strips.

2 Pour the turkey or chicken stock into a wok or large frying pan and bring to the boil. Add the turkey and cook gently for 3 minutes, or until the turkey is sealed completely, then using a slotted spoon, remove from the wok and reserve. Discard any stock.

3 Wipe the wok clean and reheat, then add the oil. When the oil is almost smoking, add the drained turkey and stir-fry for 2 minutes.

4 Add the drained mushrooms to the wok with the red pepper, the sugar snap peas and the shiitake and oyster mushrooms. Stir-fry for 2 minutes, then add the yellow bean, soy and hot chilli sauces.

5 Stir-fry the mixture for 1–2 minutes more, or until the turkey is cooked thoroughly and the vegetables are cooked but still retain a bite. Turn into a warmed serving dish and serve immediately with freshly cooked noodles.

HELPFUL HINT

Turkey is not normally associated with Chinese or Thai cuisine. However, it is now finding popularity due to its low fat content and the many cuts that are available.

THAI GREEN FRAGRANT MUSSELS

INGREDIENTS   Serves 4

2 kg/4½ lb fresh mussels
4 tbsp olive oil
2 garlic cloves, peeled and finely sliced
3 tbsp fresh root ginger, peeled and finely sliced
3 lemon grass stalks, outer leaves discarded and finely sliced
1–3 red or green chillies, deseeded and chopped

1 green pepper, deseeded and diced
5 spring onions, trimmed and finely sliced
3 tbsp freshly chopped coriander
1 tbsp sesame oil
juice of 3 limes
400 ml can coconut milk
warm crusty bread, to serve

1 Scrub the mussels under cold running water, removing any barnacles and beards. Discard any that have broken or damaged shells or are opened and do not close when tapped gently.

2 Heat a wok or large frying pan, add the oil and when hot, add the mussels. Shake gently and cook for 1 minute, then add the garlic, ginger, sliced lemon grass, chillies, green pepper, spring onions, 2 tablespoons of the chopped coriander and the sesame oil.

3 Stir-fry over a medium heat for 3–4 minutes, or until the mussels are cooked and have opened. Discard any mussels that remain unopened.

4 Pour the lime juice with the coconut milk into the wok and bring to the boil. Tip the mussels and the cooking liquor

into warmed individual bowls. Sprinkle with the remaining chopped coriander and serve immediately with warm crusty bread.

HELPFUL HINT

Mussels and other shellfish are often eaten raw in Thailand. The less they are cooked the better, as they will toughen if overcooked and lose their fresh sea flavour. Add the lime juice and coconut milk as soon as they have opened and quickly bring to the boil. Buy mussels no more than 24 hours before you need them, so that they are really fresh.

GINGER LOBSTER

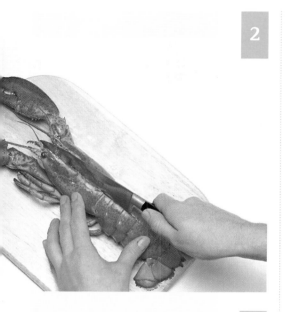

INGREDIENTS Serves 4

1 celery stalk, trimmed and finely chopped

1 onion, peeled and chopped

1 small leek, trimmed and chopped

10 black peppercorns

1 x 550 g/1¼ lb live lobster

25 g/1 oz butter

75 g/3 oz raw prawns, peeled and finely chopped

6 tbsp fish stock

50 g/2 oz fresh root ginger, peeled and cut into matchsticks

2 shallots, peeled and finely chopped

4 shiitake mushrooms, wiped and finely chopped

1 tsp green peppercorns, drained and crushed

2 tbsp oyster sauce

freshly ground black pepper

¼ tsp cornflour

sprigs of fresh coriander, to garnish

freshly cooked Thai rice and mixed shredded leek, celery, and red chilli, to serve

1 Place the celery, onion and leek in a large saucepan with the black peppercorns. Pour in 2 litres/3½ pints of hot water, bring to the boil and boil for 5 minutes, then immerse the lobster and boil for a further 8 minutes.

2 Remove the lobster. When cool enough to handle, sit it on its back. Using a sharp knife, halve the lobster neatly along its entire length. Remove and discard the intestinal vein from the tail, the stomach, (which lies near the head) and the inedible gills or dead man's fingers. Remove the meat from the shell and claws and cut into pieces.

3 Heat a wok or large frying pan, add the butter and when melted, add the raw prawns and fish stock. Stir-fry for 3 minutes

or until the prawns change colour. Add the ginger, shallots, mushrooms, green peppercorns and oyster sauce. Season to taste with black pepper. Stir in the lobster. Stir-fry for 2–3 minutes.

4 Blend the cornflour with 1 teaspoon of water to form a thick paste, stir into the wok and cook, stirring, until the sauce thickens. Place the lobster on a warmed serving platter and tip the sauce over. Garnish and serve immediately.

HELPFUL HINT

If a live lobster is unavailable, use a frozen cooked or ready-cooked lobster. Omit cooking in flavoured water, simply cut in half and proceed as above.

CRISPY AROMATIC DUCK

INGREDIENTS   Serves 4–6

2 tbsp Chinese five spice
  powder
75 g/3 oz Szechuan
  peppercorns, lightly crushed
25 g/1 oz whole black
  peppercorns, lightly crushed
3 tbsp cumin seeds, lightly
  crushed
200 g/7 oz rock salt
2.7 kg/6 lb oven-ready duck
7.5 cm/3 inch piece fresh root
  ginger, peeled and cut into 6
  slices

6 spring onions, trimmed and
  cut into 7.5 cm/3 inch lengths
cornflour for dusting
1.1 litres/2 pints groundnut oil

TO SERVE:
warm Chinese pancakes
spring onion, cut into shreds
cucumber, cut into slices
  lengthways
hoisin sauce

1 Mix together the Chinese five spice powder, Szechuan and black peppercorns, cumin seeds and salt. Rub the duck inside and out with the spice mixture. Wrap the duck with clingfilm and place in the refrigerator for 24 hours. Brush any loose spices from the duck. Place the ginger and spring onions into the duck cavity and put the duck on a heatproof plate.

2 Place a wire rack in a wok and pour in boiling water to a depth of 5 cm/2 inches. Lower the duck and plate on to the rack and cover. Steam gently for 2 hours or until the duck is cooked through, pouring off excess fat from time to time and adding more water, if necessary. Remove the duck, pour off all the liquid and discard the ginger and spring onions. Leave the duck in a cool place for 2 hours, or until it has dried and cooled.

3 Cut the duck into quarters and dust lightly with cornflour. Heat the oil in a wok or deep-fat fryer to 190°C/375°F, then deep-fry the duck quarters 2 at a time. Cook the breast for 8–10 minutes and the thighs and legs for 12–14 minutes, or until each piece is heated through. Drain on absorbent kitchen paper, then shred with a fork. Serve immediately with warm Chinese pancakes, spring onion shreds, cucumber slices and hoisin sauce.

TASTY TIP

To serve 4–6 people, you will need about 20 pancakes. Brush or spray each with a little water and a few drops of sesame oil. Layer them in a steamer on a plate and warm through for 10 minutes.

SZECHUAN SESAME CHICKEN

INGREDIENTS   Serves 4

1 medium egg white
pinch of salt
2 tsp cornflour
450 g/1 lb boneless, skinless
  chicken breast, cut into
  7.5 cm/3 inch strips
300 ml/½ pint groundnut oil
1 tbsp sesame seeds
2 tsp dark soy sauce
2 tsp cider vinegar
2 tsp chilli bean sauce

2 tsp sesame oil
2 tsp sugar
1 tbsp Chinese rice wine
1 tsp whole Szechuan
  peppercorns, roasted
2 tbsp spring onion, trimmed
  and finely chopped
mixed salad, to serve

1 Beat the egg white with a pinch of salt and the cornflour, pour into a shallow dish and add the chicken strips. Turn to coat, cover with clingfilm and leave in the refrigerator for 20 minutes.

2 Heat a wok, add the groundnut oil and when hot, add the chicken pieces and stir-fry for 2 minutes or until the chicken turns white. Using a slotted spoon, remove the chicken and drain on absorbent kitchen paper. Pour off the oil and reserve 1 tablespoon of the oil. Wipe the wok clean.

3 Reheat the wok, add 1 tablespoon of the groundnut oil with the sesame seeds and stir-fry for 30 seconds, or until golden. Stir in the dark soy sauce, cider vinegar, chilli bean sauce, sesame oil, sugar, Chinese rice wine, Szechuan peppercorns and the spring onions. Bring to the boil.

4 Return the chicken to the wok and stir-fry for 2 minutes, making sure that the chicken is coated evenly with the sauce and sesame seeds. Turn into a warmed serving dish and serve immediately with a mixed salad.

FOOD FACT

Szechuan pepper, also known as anise pepper, is actually the dried red berries of a type of ash tree. Hot and peppery, it is widely used in the spicy cuisine of the Szechuan region. It should always be roasted before use. If this has not already been done, place the 'peppercorns' on a baking tray and roast in a preheated oven at 180°C/350°F/Gas Mark 4 for 15 minutes.

SHREDDED CHILLI BEEF

INGREDIENTS   Serves 4

450 g/1 lb lean beef steak, cut into very thin strips
1 tbsp Chinese rice wine
1 tbsp light soy sauce
2 tsp sesame oil
2 tsp cornflour
8 red chillies, deseeded
8 garlic cloves, peeled
225 g/8 oz onion, peeled and sliced
1 tsp Thai red curry paste

6 tbsp groundnut oil
2 red peppers, deseeded and sliced
2 celery stalks, trimmed and sliced
2 tbsp Thai fish sauce
1 tbsp dark soy sauce
shredded basil leaves and a sprig of fresh basil, to garnish
freshly cooked noodles, to serve

1 Place the beef in a bowl with the Chinese rice wine, light soy sauce, sesame oil and cornflour and mix well. Cover with clingfilm and leave to marinate in the refrigerator for 20 minutes, turning the beef over at least once.

2 Place the chillies, garlic, onion and red curry paste in a food processor and blend to form a smooth paste.

3 Drain the beef, shaking off any excess marinade. Heat a wok and add 3 tablespoons of the groundnut oil. When almost smoking, add the beef and stir-fry for 1 minute. Using a slotted spoon, remove the beef and reserve.

4 Wipe the wok clean, reheat and add the remaining oil. When hot add the chilli paste and stir-fry for 30 seconds. Add the peppers and celery with the fish sauce and dark soy sauce. Stir-fry for 2 minutes. Return the beef to the wok and stir-fry for a further 2 minutes or until the beef is cooked. Place into a warmed serving dish, sprinkle with shredded basil and a basil sprig and serve immediately with noodles.

TASTY TIP

This recipe contains a large amount of chillies as well as Thai red curry paste, but if you prefer a less spicy dish you can reduce the quantity or chillies to 1 or 2. Choose ordinary red chillies rather than the tiny Thai ones, which would make the dish extremely hot and fiery.

PORK WITH TOFU

INGREDIENTS   Serves 4

450 g/1 lb smoked firm tofu, drained
2 tbsp groundnut oil
3 garlic cloves, peeled and crushed
2.5 cm/1 inch piece fresh root ginger, peeled and finely chopped
350 g/12 oz fresh pork mince
1 tbsp chilli powder

1 tsp sugar
2 tbsp Chinese rice wine
1 tbsp dark soy sauce
1 tbsp light soy sauce
2 tbsp yellow bean sauce
1 tsp Szechuan peppercorns
75 ml/3 fl oz chicken stock
spring onions, trimmed and finely sliced, to garnish
fried rice, to serve

1 Cut the tofu into 1 cm/½ inch cubes and place in a sieve to drain. Place the tofu on absorbent kitchen paper to dry thoroughly for another 10 minutes.

2 Heat the wok, add the groundnut oil and when hot, add the garlic and ginger. Stir-fry for a few seconds to flavour the oil, but not to colour the vegetables. Add the pork mince and stir-fry for 3 minutes, or until the pork is sealed and there are no lumps in the mince.

3 Add all the remaining ingredients except for the tofu. Bring the mixture to the boil, then reduce the heat to low. Add the tofu and mix it in gently, taking care not to break up the tofu chunks, but ensuring an even mixture of ingredients. Simmer, uncovered, for 15 minutes, or until the tofu is tender. Turn into a warmed serving dish, garnish with sliced spring onions and serve immediately with fried rice.

HELPFUL HINT

When adding spices such as garlic and ginger to hot oil, make sure you only cook them for a few seconds to develop their flavour, moving them around the pan all the time, and do not allow them to burn or they will taste bitter. When adding the pork mince, break down the lumps of meat as much as possible, so the mince is really fine.

ROYAL FRIED RICE

INGREDIENTS   Serves 4

450 g/1 lb Thai fragrant rice
2 large eggs
2 tsp sesame oil
salt and freshly ground black
  pepper
3 tbsp vegetable oil
1 red pepper, deseeded and
  finely diced
1 yellow pepper, deseeded
  and finely diced
1 green pepper, deseeded and
  finely diced
2 red onions, peeled and diced

125 g/4 oz sweetcorn kernels
125 g/4 oz cooked peeled
  prawns, thawed if frozen
125 g/4 oz white crabmeat,
  drained if canned
¼ tsp sugar
2 tsp light soy sauce

TO GARNISH:
radish roses
freshly snipped and whole
  chive leaves

1 Place the rice in a sieve, rinse with cold water, then drain. Place in a saucepan and add twice the volume of water, stirring briefly. Bring to the boil, cover and simmer gently for 15 minutes without further stirring. If the rice has fully absorbed the water while covered, add a little more water. Continue to simmer, uncovered, for another 5 minutes, or until the rice is fully cooked and the water has evaporated. Leave to cool.

2 Place the eggs, sesame oil and a pinch of salt in a small bowl. Using a fork, mix just to break the egg. Reserve.

3 Heat a wok and add 1 tablespoon of the vegetable oil. When very hot, stir-fry the peppers, onion and sweetcorn for 2 minutes or until the onion is soft. Remove the vegetables and reserve.

4 Clean the wok and add the remaining oil. When very hot, add the cold cooked rice and stir-fry for 3 minutes, or until it is heated through. Drizzle in the egg mixture and continue to stir-fry for 2–3 minutes or until the eggs have set.

5 Add the prawns and crabmeat to the rice. Stir-fry for 1 minute. Season to taste with salt and pepper and add the sugar with the soy sauce. Stir to mix and spoon into a warmed serving dish. Garnish with a radish flower and sprinkle with freshly snipped and whole chives. Serve immediately.

TASTY TIP

For more flavour cook the rice in a light unsalted chicken or vegetable stock.

CRISPY CHICKEN NOODLES

INGREDIENTS   Serves 4

1 medium egg white
2 tsp cornflour
salt and freshly ground white
  pepper
225 g/8 oz boneless and skinless
  chicken breast, diced
225 g/8 oz medium Chinese
  egg noodles
200 ml/7 fl oz groundnut oil

2 tbsp Chinese rice wine
2 tbsp oyster sauce
1 tbsp light soy sauce
300 ml/½ pint chicken stock
1 tbsp cornflour

TO GARNISH:
spring onion curls
toasted cashew nuts

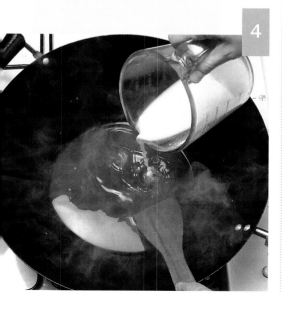

1 Mix the egg white with the cornflour in a bowl, season to taste with salt and pepper, then add the chicken and stir to coat. Chill in the refrigerator for 20 minutes. Blanch the noodles for 2 minutes in a large saucepan of boiling salted water and drain.

2 Heat a wok or large frying pan and add 2 tablespoons of the groundnut oil. When hot, spread the noodles evenly over the surface, reduce the heat to low and cook for about 5 minutes, or until browned on one side. Gently turn over, adding extra oil if necessary, and cook until both sides are browned. Reserve and keep warm.

3 Drain the chicken. Wipe the wok clean, reheat and add the remaining groundnut oil. When hot, add the chicken and stir-fry for 2 minutes. Using a slotted spoon, remove and drain on absorbent kitchen paper. Keep warm.

4 Wipe the wok clean, reheat and pour in the Chinese rice wine, oyster sauce, soy sauce and chicken stock and season lightly. Bring to the boil. Blend the cornflour to a paste with 2 tablespoons of water and stir into the wok. Cook, stirring, until the sauce has thickened. Cook for a further 1 minute.

5 Tip the noodles on to warmed plates, top with the crispy chicken pieces and drizzle over the sauce. Garnish with spring onion curls and sprinkle with toasted cashew nuts. Serve immediately.

TASTY TIP

Tossing chicken in a mixture of egg white and cornflour gives it a protective, thin crispy coating that keeps it succulent.

STIR-FRIED GREENS

INGREDIENTS
Serves 4

450 g/1 lb Chinese leaves
225 g/8 oz pak choi
225 g/8 oz broccoli florets
1 tbsp sesame seeds
1 tbsp groundnut oil
1 tbsp fresh root ginger,
    peeled and finely chopped
3 garlic cloves, peeled and
    finely chopped
2 red chillies, deseeded and
    split in half
50 ml/2 fl oz chicken stock
2 tbsp Chinese rice wine

1 tbsp dark soy sauce
1 tsp light soy sauce
2 tsp black bean sauce
freshly ground black pepper
2 tsp sugar
1 tsp sesame oil

1 Separate the Chinese leaves and pak choi and wash well. Cut into 2.5 cm/1 inch strips. Separate the broccoli into small florets. Heat a wok or large frying pan, add the sesame seeds and stir-fry for 30 seconds or until browned.

2 Add the oil to the wok and when hot, add the ginger, garlic and chillies and stir-fry for 30 seconds. Add the broccoli and stir-fry for 1 minute. Add the Chinese leaves and pak choi and stir-fry for a further 1 minute.

3 Pour the chicken stock and Chinese rice wine into the wok with the soy and black bean sauces. Season to taste with pepper and add the sugar. Reduce the heat and simmer for 6–8 minutes, or until the vegetables are tender but still firm to the

bite. Tip into a warmed serving dish, removing the chillies if preferred. Drizzle with the sesame oil and serve immediately.

FOOD FACT

Sugar is often used in Chinese and Thai cooking to round and balance flavours. Combined with vinegar, as here, it gives a sweet-and-sour flavour. Palm sugar is often used as it has a slight caramel taste and adds a golden brown colour to dishes. You can buy it from Oriental grocers, either in packets or tins. Irregular-shaped, amber-coloured coffee crystals make a good substitute or you can simply use light soft brown or demerara sugar instead.

COLOURFUL BEEF IN LETTUCE

INGREDIENTS   Serves 4

450 g/1 lb fresh beef mince
2 tbsp Chinese rice wine
1 tbsp light soy sauce
2 tsp sesame oil
2 tsp cornflour
25 g/1 oz Chinese dried
   mushrooms
2 tbsp groundnut oil
1 garlic clove, peeled and
   crushed
1 shallot, peeled and finely
   chopped
2 spring onions, trimmed and
   finely sliced
2 carrots, peeled and cut into
   matchsticks

125 g/4 oz canned bamboo
   shoots, drained and cut into
   matchsticks
2 courgettes, trimmed and cut
   into matchsticks
1 red pepper, deseeded and
   cut into matchsticks
1 tbsp dark soy sauce
2 tbsp hoisin sauce
2 tbsp oyster sauce
4 large Iceberg lettuce leaves
sprigs of fresh flat leaf parsley,
   to garnish

1 Place the beef mince in a bowl with 1 tablespoon of the Chinese rice wine, the light soy sauce, sesame oil and cornflour. Mix well and leave for 20 minutes.

2 Soak the dried mushrooms in almost boiling water for 20 minutes. Drain, rinse, drain again and squeeze out excess liquid. Trim and slice finely.

3 Heat a wok or large frying pan, add 1 tablespoon of the groundnut oil and when very hot, add the beef. Stir-fry for 1 minute, then using a slotted spoon, remove. Reserve.

4 Wipe the wok clean and reheat. Add the remaining oil and when hot, add the garlic,

shallot and spring onions and stir-fry for 10 seconds. Add the carrots and stir-fry for 1 minute. Add the mushrooms with the bamboo shoots, courgettes and pepper and stir-fry for 1 minute. Add the reserved beef, soy, hoisin and oyster sauces to the wok and stir-fry for 3 minutes.

5 Spoon the beef mixture on to lettuce leaves and fold into parcels. Garnish with flat leaf parsley sprigs and serve.

HELPFUL HINT

Use a good-quality meat for this dish, such as steak mince, and fry over a high heat so that it browns well.

COCONUT SORBET WITH MANGO SAUCE

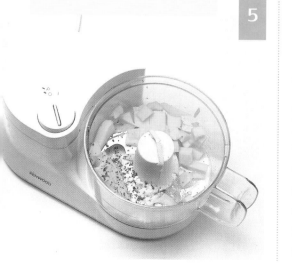

INGREDIENTS   Serves 4

2 sheets gelatine
250 g/9 oz caster sugar
600 ml/1 pint coconut milk

2 mangos, peeled, pitted and
  sliced
2 tbsp icing sugar
zest and juice of 1 lime

1 Set the freezer to rapid freeze, 2 hours before freezing the sorbet. Place the sheets of gelatine in a shallow dish, pour over cold water to cover and leave for 15 minutes. Squeeze out excess moisture before use.

2 Meanwhile, place the caster sugar and 300 ml/½ pint of the coconut milk in a heavy-based saucepan and heat gently, stirring occasionally, until the sugar has dissolved. Remove from the heat.

3 Add the soaked gelatine to the saucepan and stir gently until dissolved. Stir in the remaining coconut milk. Leave until cold.

4 Pour the gelatine and coconut mixture into a freezable container and place in the freezer. Leave for at least 1 hour, or until the mixture has started to form ice crystals. Remove and beat with a spoon, then return to the freezer and continue to freeze until the mixture is frozen, beating at least twice more during this time.

5 Meanwhile, make the sauce. Place the sliced mango, icing sugar and the lime zest and juice in a food processor and blend until smooth. Spoon into a small jug.

6 Leave the sorbet to soften in the refrigerator for at least 30 minutes before serving. Serve scoops of sorbet on individual plates with a little of the mango sauce poured over. Remember to turn the freezer to normal setting.

HELPFUL HINT

The gelatine in this cooling sorbet helps prevent large gritty ice crystals from forming as it freezes, giving it a smoother creamy texture. You can use powdered gelatine if you prefer. Sprinkle 2 level teaspoons over 2 tablespoons of cold water, leave for 5 minutes, then stir into the hot coconut milk at the beginning of step 3.

ROSE-WATER DOUGHBALLS WITH YOGURT SAUCE

INGREDIENTS   Makes 30

300 g/11 oz self-raising flour,
  sifted
50 g/2 oz ground almonds
75 g/3 oz butter, cubed
75 ml/3 fl oz natural yogurt
2 tsp rose water
grated zest of 1 orange
600 ml/1 pint vegetable oil

65 g/2½ oz caster sugar
lime zest, to decorate

FOR THE YOGURT SAUCE:
200 ml/7 fl oz natural yogurt
2 tsp rose water
grated zest of 1 lime
1 tbsp icing sugar, sifted

1 To make the yogurt sauce, blend the yogurt with the rose water, lime zest and sugar in a small bowl. Pour into a serving jug, cover with clingfilm and refrigerate until ready to serve.

2 Place the flour and ground almonds in a large bowl and, using your fingertips, rub in the butter until the mixture resembles fine breadcrumbs.

3 Add the yogurt, rose water and orange zest to the crumbed mixture, pour in 50 ml/2 fl oz of warm water and mix with a knife to form a soft pliable dough. Turn on to a lightly floured board and knead for 2 minutes or until smooth, then divide the dough into 30 small balls.

4 Heat the vegetable oil in a large wok or deep-fat fryer to 190°C/375°F, or until a bread cube dropped into the oil sizzles and turns golden brown. Working in batches of a few at a time, deep-fry the dough balls for 5–6 minutes or until golden brown. Using a slotted spoon, remove the balls from the oil and drain on absorbent kitchen paper.

5 Pour the caster sugar on a plate and roll all the dough balls in the sugar until well coated. Decorate with a little lime zest and serve immediately with the yogurt sauce.

FOOD FACT

Rose-water is a clear, fragrant liquid distilled from rose petals or from rose oil and is the flavouring used in Turkish delight. Use it sparingly as it is very powerful. Orange flower water, distilled from the flowers of Seville oranges would also work well here.

CHOCOLATE & LEMON GRASS MOUSSE

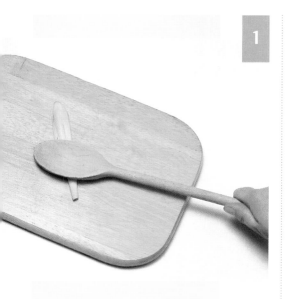

INGREDIENTS
Serves 4

3 lemon grass stalks, outer
  leaves removed
200 ml/7 fl oz milk
2 sheets gelatine
150 g/5 oz milk chocolate,
  broken into small pieces

2 medium egg yolks
50 g/2 oz caster sugar
150 ml/¼ pint double cream
juice of 2 lemons
1 tbsp caster sugar
lemon zest, to decorate

1 Use a wooden spoon to bruise the lemon grass, then cut in half. Pour the milk into a large heavy-based saucepan, add the lemon grass and bring to the boil. Remove from the heat, leave to infuse for 1 hour, then strain. Place the gelatine in a shallow dish, pour over cold water to cover and leave for 15 minutes. Squeeze out excess moisture before use.

2 Place the chocolate in a small bowl set over a saucepan of gently simmering water and leave until melted. Make sure the water does not touch the bowl.

3 Whisk the egg yolks and sugar together until thick, then whisk in the flavoured milk. Pour into a clean saucepan and cook gently, stirring continuously, until the mixture starts to thicken. Remove from the heat, stir in the melted chocolate and gelatine and leave to cool for a few minutes.

4 Whisk the double cream until soft peaks form, then stir into the cooled milk mixture to form a mousse. Spoon into individual ramekins or moulds and leave in the refrigerator for 2 hours or until set.

5 Just before serving, pour the lemon juice into a small saucepan, bring to the boil, then simmer for 3 minutes or until reduced. Add the sugar and heat until dissolved, stirring continuously. Serve the mousse drizzled with the lemon sauce and decorated with lemon zest.

HELPFUL HINT

Take care when melting milk chocolate not to overheat it; the water in the pan should be barely bubbling and it is a good idea to turn off the heat as soon as the chocolate begins to melt. Buy chocolate specifically for desserts and baking, but avoid chocolate-flavoured cake covering.

COCONUT RICE SERVED WITH STEWED GINGER FRUITS

INGREDIENTS   Serves 6–8

1 vanilla pod
450 ml/¾ pint coconut milk
1.1 litres/2 pints semi-
    skimmed milk
600 ml/1 pint double cream
100 g/3½ oz caster sugar
2 star anise
8 tbsp toasted desiccated
    coconut
250 g/9 oz short-grain pudding
    rice

1 tsp melted butter
2 mandarin oranges, peeled
    and pith removed
1 star fruit, sliced
50 g/2 oz stem ginger, finely
    diced
300 ml/½ pint sweet white
    wine
caster sugar, to taste

1 Preheat the oven to 160°C/ 325°F/Gas Mark 3. Using a sharp knife, split the vanilla pod in half lengthways, scrape out the seeds from the pods and place both the pod and seeds in a large heavy-based casserole dish. Pour in the coconut milk, the semi-skimmed milk and the double cream and stir in the sugar, star anise and 4 tablespoons of the toasted coconut. Bring to the boil, then simmer for 10 minutes, stirring occasionally. Remove the vanilla pod and star anise.

2 Wash the rice and add to the milk. Simmer gently for 25–30 minutes or until the rice is tender, stirring frequently. Stir in the melted butter.

3 Divide the mandarins into segments and place in a saucepan with the sliced star fruit and stem ginger. Pour in the white wine and 300 ml/½ pint water, bring to the boil, then reduce the heat and simmer for 20 minutes or until the liquid has reduced and the fruits softened. Add sugar to taste.

4 Serve the rice, topped with the stewed fruits and the remaining toasted coconut.

FOOD FACT

Star fruit, or carambola, is a pale yellow-green fruit with a pretty star-shaped appearance when cut horizontally. It is almost flavourless with just a hint of sweet and sour and has a crunchy texture when eaten raw. Poaching it in white wine and ginger makes it taste as good as it looks.

PASSION FRUIT & POMEGRANATE CITRUS TART

INGREDIENTS   Serves 4

FOR THE PASTRY:
175 g/6 oz plain flour
pinch of salt
125 g/4 oz butter
4 tsp caster sugar
1 small egg, separated

FOR THE FILLING:
2 passion fruit
175 g/6 oz caster sugar
4 large eggs
175 ml/6 fl oz double cream
3 tbsp lime juice
1 pomegranate
icing sugar for dusting

1 Preheat the oven to 200°C/ 400°F/Gas Mark 6. Sift the flour and salt into a large bowl and rub in the butter until the mixture resembles fine breadcrumbs. Stir in the sugar.

2 Whisk the egg yolk and add to the dry ingredients. Mix well to form a smooth, pliable dough. Knead gently on a lightly floured surface until smooth. Wrap the pastry and leave to rest in the refrigerator for 30 minutes.

3 Roll out the pastry on a lightly floured surface and use to line a 25.5 cm/10 inch loose-based flan tin. Line the pastry case with greaseproof paper and baking beans. Brush the edges of the pastry with the egg white and bake blind in the preheated oven for 15 minutes. Remove the paper and beans and bake for 5 minutes. Remove and reduce the temperature to 180°C/350°F/Gas Mark 4.

4 Halve the passion fruit and spoon the flesh into a bowl. Whisk the sugar and eggs together in a bowl. When mixed thoroughly, stir in the double cream with passion fruit juice and flesh and the lime juice.

5 Pour the mixture into the pastry case and bake for 30–40 minutes or until the filling is just set. Remove and cool slightly, then chill in the refrigerator for 1 hour. Cut the pomegranate in half and scoop the seeds into a sieve. Spoon the drained seeds over the top and just before serving dust with icing sugar.

HELPFUL HINT

Pomegranates have leathery skin and may be a dark yellow to a crimson colour. They have a distinctive slightly acidic flavour.

INDEX